CHARLEY

The True Story of the Youngest Soldier to
Die in the American Civil War

D1715264

BRENDAN J. LYONS

Maddie,
Enjoy!

Brendan J. Lyons

BROOKLINE
books
Havertown, Pennsylvania

Brookline Books is an imprint of Casemate Publishers

Published in the United States of America and Great Britain in 2023 by
CASEMATE PUBLISHERS
1950 Lawrence Road, Havertown, PA 19083, USA
and
The Old Music Hall, 106–108 Cowley Road, Oxford OX4 1JE, UK

Paperback Edition: ISBN 978-1-95504-106-5
Digital Edition: ISBN 978-1-95504-107-2

A CIP record for this book is available from the British Library

Printed and bound in the United Kingdom by CPI Group (UK) Ltd, Croydon, CR0 4YY

For a complete list of Brookline Books titles, please contact:

CASEMATE PUBLISHERS (US)
Telephone (610) 853-9131
Fax (610) 853-9146
Email: casemate@casematepublishers.com
www.casematepublishers.com

CASEMATE PUBLISHERS (UK)
Telephone (0)1226 734350
Email: casemate-uk@casematepublishers.co.uk
www.casematepublishers.co.uk

Cover image: Charley. (Robert S. Westbrook, History of the 49th Pennsylvania Volunteers
(Altoona, PA: Altoona Time Print, 1898))

Contents

12 YEARS 5 MO. AND 9 DAYS.
OLD WHEN HE ENLISTED.

CHARLEY KING.

No reliable record of Charley's birth exists today, but Westbrook's account marks Charley's enlistment as occurring on September 12, 1861. If the estimate of 12 years, 5 months and 9 days is accurate, he would have born on April 3, 1849. Interestingly, the handwritten ledger used at the time of enlistment lists Charley as 18 years of age. Westbrook's account rectifies this, but one does wonder why such a preposterous age would be listed when a soldier need not be 18 years of age to enlist. (Robert S. Westbrook, *History of the 49th Pennsylvania Volunteers* (Altoona, PA: Altoona Time Print, 1898), 125)

Foreword

I first learned about Charley King when I was a 17-year-old Boy Scout in Chester County. I was looking for an Eagle Scout Project that reflected my interest in history at the time. Bob McGonigal, scout leader and member of the Sons of Union Veterans, brought the story of Charley King to my attention and I was fascinated. There was even less known about him then than is known now. We knew how old he was when he enlisted, that he was a very talented drummer, and that nobody knew where he was buried.

For my Eagle project, we decided to raise money for a monument to Charley King in recognition of his service. Since we did not know where his body lay, we decided to place the monument in Greenmount Cemetery with his family. With the help of the Sons of Union Veterans chapter in West Chester and a number of other historically minded individuals, we were able to raise enough money for the monument. My troop and I laid the walkway, created the foundation, and prepared the grounds. Charley was even given a flag holder to signify his service. The dedication on the monument is based on the obituary printed in the local West Chester newspaper.

That was over a decade ago, and Charley has never entirely left my mind. The small hand I had in honoring his bravery has never quite felt like enough, and while his story has been told, it has not—in my opinion—been told with the level of fidelity that it deserves. The truth is, we don't know a lot about what happened directly to Charley after he left West Chester, but there are things we do know.

We know the actions he was involved in as part of Company F of the 49th Pennsylvania Volunteers. We know the names of those who stood by his side, the battles he fought in, the successes he saw, and the failures he suffered.

And we know he was a very brave and passionate boy.

The story you are about to read was written with the greatest devotion to the truth possible. The names of his family, his fellow soldiers, and his officers, are all names of real people Charley would have known and probably have been close to. Their lives are presented to the best of my ability. Many of the events of his tenure with the army are drawn from the account of Sergeant Robert S. Westbrook. He compiled the journals of several soldiers in the 49th, chiefly Christian Dale, of Old Companies G and C; A. T. Hilands, of Old Companies H and A; George Wills, of Old Companies D and B; T. H. McFarland, of Old Companies D and B; Henry B. Minnichan, of Old Companies I and A; Samuel H. Philips, of Old Companies H and A; Samuel F. Enslow, Old Company I; and W. H. Mauger, Old Companies I and A, as well as several other fellow soldiers not named by Sgt. Westbrook. These accounts were vetted for accuracy against other widely accepted sources.

The rest, that which is not known, is from my heart and my desire to honor the life of Charley King, as well as the lives of the other valiant dead.

It should be noted, particularly for younger readers, that some of the language used in this book is not and should not be considered acceptable today. It was included in the speech of some characters to accurately reflect the attitudes of the people of the time.

CHAPTER I

West Chester

The first rays of sun snaked down the streets of West Chester to find Charley King already alert and awaiting the day. He knew better than to make his way downstairs before he heard his parents stirring, so he sat patiently. An uncommon excitement hung in the air for a Wednesday in April, but these were uncommon times—not only for Charley, but for the nation as a whole.

On this Wednesday in April, one month after the inauguration of President Abraham Lincoln, the nation stood on the brink of conflict.

On this Wednesday in April, as the country was coming apart at the seams because of the growing tide of secession, unprecedented animosity divided the nation that first brought the concepts of free and equal representation to the world.

On this Wednesday in April 1861, Charley King was turning twelve years old.

To the nation, these tides pushed with unequal might against the seams of time, but in one small room on the one hundred block of Barnard Street in West Chester, Pennsylvania, the election, secession, and Charley's twelfth birthday were of equal significance and their confluence was a matter of fate. At this time, when America faced its greatest test since the very revolution that created it, Charley had reached the age that—by his judgement—qualified him to stand and fight for his nation. Whether his father would agree remained to be seen, but in Charley's mind, he could lift a rifle as well as anyone and his home needed stout defenders.

Charley could see himself quite easily, decked in Union blue and marching beside his countrymen. He was already accomplished at keeping time, by virtue of his skill on the drum. His father often claimed Charley had been drumming perfect military cadence since before he could walk. Whether or not that was true, Charley couldn't say, but he certainly loved to play his drum.

Apparently, he loved to play it a tad too much and had just recently drummed right through the head of his snare. It happened two weeks earlier and, since then, he'd had to make do with whatever he could get away with drumming on. Usually, that meant a fence, tree, or wooden step. Occasionally, if no one was nearby, he could drum on a table, but he would have to do so cautiously at the risk of leaving telltale scuff marks.

With the drum beat in his mind, however, he was able to mark time perfectly around his room and, as he did, envision a future where his deeds brought glory to his family and his nation. One day—and Charley felt that day would come soon—he would find himself marching into Richmond alongside his fellow Union soldiers as streams of confetti and other colorful paper rained down on them. They would be celebrated as liberators from the wicked grasp of traitors and the people would love them for it.

The celebration would be even greater when he returned home a hero. His parents would hug him tight and say how proud they were of him. All of West Chester would come out to celebrate. Perhaps all of Chester County!

Those days of glory were coming and coming fast. First, however, Charley would have to go to school.

With a sigh, he rose to his feet and walked to his bedroom door quietly so as not to disturb his siblings. He could finally hear his mother moving about in the kitchen and felt it safe to venture downstairs. Slipping into the corridor, he scampered down the steps with his sticks in hand. Once he reached the bottom, he stood at attention and held his drumsticks out so that they hovered an inch beyond each of his legs. After holding for a moment, he began to strike his legs with the sticks in the rhythm of reveille.

Ra-tum-tata-tum-tata-tum, ra-ta-ta-ta-ta-ta-ta-tum, ra-ta-ta-ta-ta-ta-ta-ta-ta-tum.

He continued for nearly five minutes, rousing the imaginary troops from their sleep, and then went back to attention. From the kitchen, he could hear his mother working on breakfast and decided to make his way there. Holding his sticks, he signaled the right face.

Tum. Ra-tum.

He took two steps, and then again.

Tum. Ra-tum.

Then, after counting out the beat, he began to mark time before striding forward in a full parade march toward the kitchen.

Ra-ta-ta-tut-tut tut-tut-tut ra-ta-ta-ta-ta-ta-ta-ta-ta rut-tut-tut.

He reached the kitchen in a few short steps and prepared to mark time once more, his imaginary company halting beside him. As he did, his mother looked up from her work and shook her head.

"Parade rest, Charley," she said with a chuckle.

"I can't parade rest until I've halted, Mother," Charley replied, still moving his legs.

"You aren't halted?" his mother asked. "You don't appear to be moving to me. Doesn't that mean you've halted?"

Charley shook his head, keeping his eyes front as best he could.

"No, ma'am. I've stopped marching, but I am still marking time. When it's time to halt I will stand still and then I can be ordered to parade rest. But I can't go from marking time to parade rest!"

The gruff voice of his father, Pennell, cut in from behind him.

"Then halt, boy," his father said. "And parade rest and dismissed. I've got breakfast to eat and then trousers to sew and you're blocking up the way to the kitchen."

In three swift, yet distinct moves, Charley came to attention, dropped to parade rest, and then broke ranks. Hurrying to the kitchen table, he took his seat and sat up as straight as he could. His father followed, walking up to his mother and giving her a kiss on the cheek.

"Adaline, dear, would you mind making me an extra egg this morning? I had two extra orders for coats come in as I was closing up last night and I fear I'll be engaged in their preparation well into the afternoon. Last night's dinner did not sit well with my stomach, I fear—through no fault of yours, of course."

"Of course, dear," Adaline replied. "You've not taken ill, have you Pennell?"

"Certainly not," Pennell said, "merely a bit of indigestion, I am sure."

Charley's father took a seat at the table across from Charley and awaited his breakfast. Still sitting as rigidly as he could, Charley waited for his father to address him. In the meantime, he eyed the back of the paper his father was examining. The story his father was reading was, no doubt, about the troubles in the South, but Charley was relegated to reading some local story about an injured mule turning up on Wealthy Hill that ought not have been there. This would have passed as worthy news a year or so earlier, but not today.

After a few minutes, Adaline laid breakfast on the table for both Pennell and Charley.

"I'm off to wake the rest of the children, then."

"Thank you, dear," Pennell said. "Breakfast looks splendid as always."

As she left the kitchen, the Kings' next oldest son, Lewis, hurried in, slipping between her and the archway.

"Morning, Mum," he said. "I'm famished!"

"Morning, dear. Go on then."

Lewis hurried to the table and stood tall in front of Pennell.

"Morning, Father," he said. Pennell looked over his paper at him and nodded, then Lewis took his seat. Once he had filled his plate, he looked at Charley through narrowed eyes.

"*You* were supposed to wake me this morning. Mother said so."

"You're going to have to learn to wake up on your own," Charley replied. "I can. I wake up just before the dawn every morning like a good soldier should."

"But you're older than me!" Lewis protested. "Two whole years!"

Charley shook his head.

"That's nothing. Now eat up, or I'll have to leave for school without you."

Lewis looked as though he might protest to their father, but even he knew better than to disturb Pennell at breakfast. Instead, the three of them ate in silence for a few minutes, enjoying the fried potatoes and eggs. Delicious as it was, Charley was anxious for his father to speak to him about the goings on in the South. Often times, Pennell would have a word or two about the traitorous dealings of the southern states, but for some odd reason he remained silent this morning. Finally, when Charley thought he could stand the silence no more, his father spoke.

"Shameful dealings in Dixie these days," he muttered. Charley sprung on the opportunity to reply.

"More secessions this week, Father?" he asked.

"Nothing new," his father replied, "Though the rumblings from Virginia continue to grow louder. Part of me wishes they would just hop off the blasted fence already."

"Perhaps they won't secede?" Charley offered.

"I think that unlikely," his father said. "The Virginians have placed their eggs in the 'states rights' basket. If they were to balk now when the fervor is at its highest, I'm certain they would never live it down. No, I expect they're waiting for the powder keg to explode before they make their move."

Charley nodded, though he could not say he truly understood the complexities of the issue. He enjoyed listening to his father speak on it, however. It pleased him to think his father thought him worthy of talking to about such a serious thing. Charley wondered if his twelfth birthday would unlock an even greater amount of esteem.

"I heard some men saying that, if Virginia goes, Maryland will follow," Charley said, hoping to keep the conversation alive. "Do you think that's the case?"

"I should think not," Pennell replied, "much as they might want to. Lincoln would not allow such a thing. If Maryland secedes, the capital is surrounded on all sides. No, I should think Mr. Lincoln would march troops into Annapolis and Baltimore if they tried. Besides, the governor would not allow such a thing either. It's of no concern."

Charley nodded. His father was right, he assumed. Mr. Lincoln did not seem like the sort of man that would be so foolish as to let the capital be surrounded. Some claimed he was the most intelligent President ever elected. Others claimed he was a bumbling Kentucky hayseed who stumbled into power at the worst possible time, but such folks were mostly Democrats and, as such, their opinions were hardly of any merit.

"Do you think the fighting will start soon, Father?" Charley asked, as he had done countless mornings in the past. His father sighed, though he had to have known that the question would soon come. Laying his fork upon his plate, Pennell shrugged as his face fell.

"Charley, I am no soothsayer, nor can I guess the works of other men's minds. I have little doubt the war will begin, but I cannot say when or how. This is knowledge that cannot be known but by God and perhaps Mr. Lincoln. I would not trouble yourself with speculation."

"But I want to be ready when it happens," Charley said. "The first men to join have already left to prepare for battle. When it comes to war, the nation will need me."

"The nation will need men, Charley," his father replied, "not eleven-year-old boys."

"I'm twelve, Father!" Charley shot back. "It's my birthday today!"

Pennell allowed a coy smile.

"Is it?" he said. Charley's frustration turned quickly to good humor.

"You knew," Charley replied. "You should not joke with me like that, Father. One might suspect you did not know the birth date of your oldest child."

"I suppose that would not cast me in a preferable light, no. But if a father cannot make merry at the expense of his son, then what has this world come to?"

Charley rolled his eyes, but he noticed that his father's expression became serious once more.

"Now, boy, I must say—eleven, twelve, or even fifteen, I think it not wise for you to wish to go to war. Truthfully, I will not allow it. Your passion is commendable, but it would be far too dangerous. You are much too young, and besides quite slight for your age. I think you are perhaps the smallest boy in your class, Charley. You cannot go to war."

"But Father…"

"I will speak no more on this," Pennell cut in. "I must be off, and you must go to aid your mother in rousing your siblings. Focus on your studies, Charley. Think not on war."

With that, Pennell rose to his feet and gathered his things. He called up to Adaline to bid her farewell and then hurried out the door. Charley brooded as he gathered the spent dishes and moved them to the empty basin. His father was right about his size, though he was not the smallest in his class. Still, he thought his small stature wholly irrelevant to his ability to fight. If he could hold and fire a gun, he ought to be able to fight for his country.

For now, he would have to focus on other things. He did as his father said and helped his mother with the other children. Then, once they were all situated, he headed out toward the schoolhouse.

"You shouldn't argue with Father like that," Lewis said. "Mother told us that what he says is final."

"I'm not a child anymore," Charley shot back. "There is so much going on in the world and I am ready to be a part of it. I wouldn't expect a little kid like you to understand that."

"Hey, I… I could fight," Lewis said.

"You're too young," Charley replied, and lengthened his stride to head out in front of his brother. It was a rather short walk to the schoolhouse, but Charley was able to practice more on the way. Other school children hurried past him, but he maintained a steady beat as he marched in time to his own drumming.

He did not stop drumming on his legs until he reached the front door of the schoolhouse and stepped inside. Most of his class was already present and he hurriedly stuffed his sticks into his pack and went to his seat. A few of his classmates whispered "happy birthday" to him as he passed, and he smiled in thanks.

It was not a large class and, in years to come, it would likely only get smaller. The children of farmers especially would soon forgo lessons in exchange for long days in the fields. In fact, it was already rare to see such children in the school. Most of who was left were the children of shopkeepers, lawyers, or other occupations that did not require many hands. Still, they too would soon leave school in favor of apprenticeships or menial work. This was simply a fact of life. Perhaps one or two might go on to a nearby university, but that was quite rare.

For Charley's part, he had not thought much about what he would do when his time at school had ended. He might follow his father into the tailor shop, but Lewis was already far more interested in such things and only so many tailors could work in one small town. In truth, it did not interest him much, and anyway, even before the war he had not considered any profession further than a cursory interest. Now, of course, only one thing interested him.

Looking down at the sticks poking out of his bag, he thought, *well, two things*.

The lessons for that day may well have been in Greek as far as Charley was concerned. There was a brief mention of his birthday and a short round of applause, but outside of that he might as well not have come. He liked school, in general, but at this moment the world outside the schoolhouse walls was far more interesting than anything he could learn inside them. What was the point of talking about Romans, Greeks, and other peoples when they themselves stood on the cusp of history?

Charley saw little point at all.

By the time the day's end came, Charley could barely keep his feet from tapping. He was prepared to leap out of his chair and sprint home to see what news may have come while lessons were being taught, but he was stopped by a group of friends before he could.

"Where are you headed, Charley?" one of them asked.

"Oh, just going home. I thought I'd stop by the telegraph office and see if there was any war news on the way."

"Are you marching down?" asked another.

"I… I guess I can…" Charley wasn't sure where this line of questions was going. The other kids were his friends, but they rarely showed interest in his marching about anymore. It was odd that they would ask him now.

"Why don't you lead us?" the first classmate asked. "We figure if the war's gonna happen maybe we all better get in top shape, right?"

Charley frowned.

"I guess, only… I can't really lead you guys. My drum is broken."

A voice behind him made Charley jump.

"Well, I guess you'll need a new drum!"

Charley whirled around to see his parents standing there side by side, huge smiles on their faces. His father held out a large, cylindrical package.

"Happy birthday, Charley," he said.

"We hope you like it," his mother added.

Without hesitating, Charley took the package and tore off the paper. Inside, was a large blue snare drum with red trim on the top and bottom. Around the middle, it was emblazoned with a soaring bald eagle on opposite sides of the drum.

"This is amazing," Charley gasped. "It's perfect... the eagle, is this...?"

"The very drum that the musicians in the Army of the Potomac play," Pennell confirmed.

"Your father had the Sweney boy send one in," Adaline said. "He made such a show about having all that extra work so you wouldn't think anything odd if you saw him rushing about. I told him you wouldn't notice, but he does so like to play games."

"Alright, Adaline," Pennell said, "we'd better let young Charley enjoy his new drum."

"Just be home in time for supper, Charley," his mother added. "We'll have a special meal all made up for you. Run along with your friends now."

Charley's mother kissed him on the cheek and then turned away. His father gave him a nod and a wink and then followed after her. When they had left, the other children crowded around Charley to get a look at his new drum.

"Give it a roll, Charley," someone said. Strapping the drum over his shoulder, Charley pulled out his sticks and slung the drum to the right side of his body. He came to attention and let out a long, loud roll.

The other children cheered and then quickly formed into ranks to Charley's left. With a smile, he struck the drum twice, with a roll at the end.

Tut-tut-tatut.

Indicating a left face. It took the children a moment, but they were able to follow the order. Lewis fell in beside his brother with a wide smile. Charley marked time for a few moments and then led them off. Townsfolk stopped and watched as the company of children marched down the street from the schoolhouse to the telegram office with Charley drumming the cadence.

Some smiled and waved to the boys, while others shook their heads. One or two older men stopped and watched with far-away looks in their eyes. This caught Charley's attention more than the others, but he did not focus on them long. He needed to keep the cadence going and his company in line. That was the drummer's job, after all. There was no time to ponder odd looks from men he did not know.

When the company reached the telegraph office, Charley called them to a halt. Such was the commotion of their approach that the telegraph officer had already come out to see what it was about. Hands on his hips, he shook his head at them.

"Now, what's all this about?" he said.

"We've come to see if there is any news of the goings on in the South, sir," Charley answered.

"Goings on, eh," the officer replied. "Well, lemme see... not much, I'm afraid. Mr. Lincoln made a speech. We'll be getting the text of that in a few days. Word is secession is still being hotly contested in Virginia. Not much else, I'm afraid."

"Very well," Charley said, "thank you, good sir!"

"Obliged," the officer said, and returned inside.

"Ah well," Charley sighed when he had disappeared, "I suppose we shall have to wait to use this training. We could use some time to get things perfect, anyway."

"Alright," Lewis said, "what shall we do next then?"

"Hm," Charley replied, "why don't we march a few blocks down and then head toward the courthouse?"

There was a cheer of approval and then everyone came to attention. The children marched about West Chester for the better part of an hour before the first of them grew weary of it. They said their goodbyes as Charley and those who remained continued on. As the minutes passed, more decided they were done marching and wished Charley a happy birthday. Finally, it was only Charley and Lewis left. At that point, the sun had begun to sink in the sky, and he realized it was time to head home for dinner. Signaling the retreat, he double-timed his way back to Barnard Street with Lewis calling for him to slow down.

The rest of the family was waiting for him when he returned. Drum still strapped over his shoulder, Charley made his way into the kitchen where dinner was already being laid out.

"No drums at the table, Charley," his mother said.

Charley unslung his drum and placed it in the corner of the room. His father gave him a brief disapproving look and Charley hurried to move it, but Pennell just laughed.

"For today, Charley, it can stay down here. In the future, though, I expect it to be either in your room or over your shoulder. Is that understood?"

"Yes, Father," Charley replied. He took his seat as the last of the food reached the table. The family said grace and they began to dish out dinner, starting with the youngest children.

"So, you like the drum," Pennell said, as he distributed chunks of cornbread.

"I love it," Charley answered. "I led practically the whole school around town, and they all marched in line. Well, sort of a line..."

"Oh, we heard," Adaline said.

"People were talking about it?" Charley asked.

"No, your mother means we *actually* heard it," Pennell clarified. "That is quite the loud drum. Necessarily so, of course, as it must be heard over the sounds of battle."

"Hey yeah," Charley said, a thought forming in his mind. He looked over at his drum and thought about what a thrill it had been to lead his peers. And he was a good drummer—everyone said so.

"What if I was a drummer boy?" he blurted out.

"I would say you already are," his mother replied.

"No, I mean, when the war starts. The army needs drummers don't they, to help with the march and all sorts of things? But drummers don't carry guns."

Charley watched as his father drew a long breath, lying down his silverware beside his plate.

"Son, we already talked about this. You're too young. Whether you're carrying a gun or not, you would still be in danger."

"But they wouldn't fire on a drummer boy, would they?"

"The drummer marches in line with the rest of his company, Charley. Side-by-side. When one line fires on another, they are rarely discerning when it comes to their target. You are only twelve years old."

"But when I'm older? When I'm sixteen perhaps?"

"The war is not going to last that long," his father replied. "And besides, even then I think it would be unwise for you to go to war. In the mad event this war lasts four whole years, I will likely have been pulled in. Your mother cannot lose both of us."

Charley frowned, but he could see there was no use fighting his father's will. Perhaps over time he could wear him down, but tonight was not the night to convince him. He would have to bide his time.

There was no further talk of war the rest of the evening, as the family finished their dinner and celebrated Charley's birthday. As the hour grew late, Adaline put the smaller children to bed, one-by-one, until it was time for Charley to retire as well. He said goodnight to his parents, thanked them again for the drum, and went off to bed.

Now left alone in the family living room, Pennell and Adaline reclined by the small fire Charley had built after dinner.

"I do not think we have heard the last of this drummer boy talk," Adaline said, stroking her husband's face with her hand. "I fear he may drive you mad with it."

"Oh, I am under no illusion that the subject is finished," Pennell replied. "But it is not me I am worried about. It is you I fear for."

Adaline frowned.

"You truly believe that you will have to go?"

"I don't know," Pennell said. "I have no great desire to go into battle, but I will not see this nation that raised me torn asunder by rebellion. This war may be short, but it will rage with a heat hitherto unfelt in this land. There is far too much animosity between North and South for anything less."

"The thought frightens me," Adaline replied. "Though, I think perhaps it ought to. You are right. Charley will not give up on this dream."

"Sooner or later," Pennell said, "I'm afraid it will be I who wears down. He is..."

Pennell paused as a soft rapping sound fell upon his ears. Adaline heard it as well, turning her face toward the stairs that led up to the bedrooms.

"What is that?" she said.

Pennell rose to his feet.

"I have an idea."

Walking quietly up the steps, he stopped by Charley's door and peered in through the small space where it was left cracked open. There, sitting up at his bed, was Charley with his drumsticks, marking time on the headboard.

It was then Pennell knew for certain that, no matter what he said, the day would soon come that Charley marched to war.

CHAPTER 2

Fort Sumter

By the afternoon of April 14, many of the neighborhood children had lost interest in marching about, but Charley still practiced constantly. On that particular day, only two of his classmates had decided to join him and he was leading them in wheeling turns around a cross-street. Some of the townsfolk were still in their Sunday best but the children had already changed into play clothes. Charley had assembled an outfit comprised entirely of blue, though not entirely the same shade. He had encouraged the other children to do likewise, but they did not possess the same level of dedication as he did.

Charley had also attempted to convince several different children to take up the fife and bugle so that they could form their own music corps, but they showed little interest in doing so. Lewis briefly considered an instrument but decided that he wanted to play the drum like Charley, a proposition his brother flatly rejected. Frustrated by the lack of real commitment from the other children, Charley redoubled his own enthusiasm to make up for it.

His small company was marching down toward High Street when they heard a commotion at the telegraph office. Without a moment's hesitation, Charley signaled the left turn and they hurried off in double-time. People were gathering from several blocks away to hear whatever news had just come in. The children came to a halt a short distance from the office and dismissed themselves without the proper drumbeat. Normally Charley would have protested, but he was just as curious about what might be happening.

"What's going on?" Charley shouted to one of his neighbors who had just rushed out of the office. "Is there news about the coming war?"

"It isn't coming anymore," his neighbor replied. "It's here. The Rebels have taken Fort Sumter. It fell yesterday to General Beauregard."

"Fort Sumter," Lewis said. "Where is that?"

"South Carolina," Charley answered. "It's right outside of Charleston. Mr. Lincoln just announced he planned to resupply the fort after the southerners started seceding. Don't you read the paper?"

"Charley's got it right," the neighbor said. "That fort guards the harbor. Those Carolina boys would have had quite the time getting ships in and out had that fort held out. I suppose Old Abe's going to have to blockade the port now—not like we don't have the ships, of course."

Charley thought over what his neighbor had said for a few moments before asking,

"Do you think that means the war might last longer than people are saying? Since we lost the first battle and all?"

"Well, I don't know if I'd say that," his neighbor replied. "A port's just a port. It isn't like you can ship in military organization and good old northern know-how. No, at worst this is a tiny set-back. Mr. Lincoln will wipe them off the field the first time our troops meet theirs face to face. You can count on that."

Charley frowned, but he supposed his neighbor was probably right. The South was nothing but farmers and slaves, not like the North. They had factories, big cities, and fierce generals to lead them. And, of course, the North had Mr. Lincoln.

"I better get back to my parents," one of Charley's classmates said, interrupting his thoughts. "They'll wanna know about this if they don't already."

"But we've only just started our drills," Charley protested.

"Sorry," another classmate said. "Maybe you ought to go home, too. I'm sure your Mom and Pop are gonna wanna see you. Do you think they'll let you be a drummer boy after all?"

"Probably not," Charley said. "They say I'm too young. And anyway, if the war's gonna be over after the first battle, I guess there's not much point. Maybe I'll drum for the next war, I dunno."

"Maybe," his classmate replied. "Anyway, I'll be seeing ya."

Charley waved goodbye to his classmates and his neighbors, and headed back home, marking time on his drum as he went. He kept a steady beat, but he didn't much feel like marching. History was happening with every passing moment, and it was happening without him. He wondered if boys his age played drums during the Revolution, or how many had to stay home and miss their chance at building a new nation. Now Charley had a chance to save that new nation, but there was nothing he could do.

As he walked, Charley changed his cadence to one of an advancing line of troops. He pictured that first battle, the great conflict that so many were certain would quickly decide the war. Cannon balls flew by him, whizzing over his head as he kept perfect time, never allowing any danger to cause him to flinch. No bullets, no shot, no explosions could distract him from guiding his fellow soldiers.

And guide them he would—over the field, face-to-face with the enemy, and charging into the Rebel ranks with reckless abandon. No man would fall behind with Charley at the drum. Every single soldier moved in unison thanks to his clear, sharp strikes and thundering rolls. Even over the din of ten thousand rifles, he could be heard drumming out orders as his captain shouted them. It was what he was meant for—the task he was born for.

But he was too young.

He greatly doubted there was any way he could change his parents' minds. While he did not begrudge them for wanting to keep him safe, he struggled with the thought that others not much older than him would be going off to fight any day now. Even his father might be asked to enlist and fight against the Rebels. And he would be left behind to help his mother.

As he rounded the corner to his own block, he saw her waiting on the porch. He could see worry etched upon her face. She must have already heard about the battle.

"Hello, Charley," she said, as he approached. "Did you have a fun day today? It sounded like you were having quite the time. I could hear you drumming all over town. Not that that is any different from most days."

His mother donned a whimsical, distant look Charley had not seen before and sighed.

"I always know just when school is let out, when you're headed our way, or when you are marching off to the other side of town. Some mothers worry about where their boy has gone. I'm lucky. I can always hear mine."

"Are you alright, Mother?" Charley asked. "You seem, um, sad…"

"I'm alright, Charley," she replied. "I suppose I just thought there might be a chance that the war would never come. That, perhaps, we might find another compromise to keep our nation together. I guess the men in Washington ran out of ideas. Or maybe just ran out of patience. Maybe it was a little bit of both."

"Do you think Father is gonna have to go fight?" Charley asked. "Do you think they'll make him join the army? It doesn't seem like he really wants to."

"I'm not certain he'll have a choice," Charley's mother said. "But I do know that if his nation needs him, he will not hesitate to fight for it. He was a lot like you when he was younger, and I still see that fire in him from time to time. When something is right, he is willing to put his life on the line to defend it. Of that, I am certain."

Charley looked down at his feet, reflecting on his mother's words.

"I want to be like that," he said, confident the feeling was just. "And this isn't just anything. This is our country. And this is people. I want to stand up for what is right in any way I can. We talked in class the other day, about how our country got to this point. So much has gone into making us who we are, and so many people have fought to build what we have. I don't know why anyone would want to throw that away.

"But one of my classmates, he's got family in the South. Well, he says his cousins think the same thing, only they don't think we're talking about people. Way they see it, they've got the rights our founders promised, but that wasn't meant for the black folks. I'm not sure how they can think a black person isn't a person. I suppose they think they're a different kind of person?"

"Even that's a dangerous thought," came Pennell's voice from behind. Charley whirled around to see him just a few steps away.

"Did you hear?" he asked his father. Pennell nodded, but he hadn't finished his thought from before.

"Charley, there's a lot of different people in this world. Truth be told, I've only met a handful of black folks in my time. I can't say I understand a thing about 'em, but they don't seem like a different *type* of person to me—just a person. Now, if one of them walked into my place of business and said he's new up from the South and looking for a job... well. I guess I can't say what I'd do."

"Hire him?" Charley said, "provided he can do the job."

Charley's father smiled, but it looked strained. Something about the idea caused him a struggle, but Charley couldn't place it. Whatever it was, there was no way for him to find out, as his father quickly changed the subject.

"I did hear about Fort Sumter," Pennell said. "I suppose the war has started in earnest—no longer a struggle of words, thoughts, and ideas. We're on to a struggle of blood, bullets, and bodies."

"Mr. Gardener said missing the chance to take the Port of Charleston might make the war be longer," Charley said, doing his best to hide his excitement. "Do you think he's right about that?"

Pennell frowned.

"Horace said that? Well, I can't say, but I still believe our army will be overwhelming. Remember, the fort was lightly occupied and in Southern territory. When it comes to the field, there will not be the same advantage for the Rebels."

Pennell watched his son's face fall and shook his head.

"Listen, son," he said, "I know you believe in Mr. Lincoln's cause, and you are right for being passionate about our nation, but war is never something to be hoped for. In war, a bullet will find a just man as easily as it will an unjust man. Good men and evil men alike die in war—have died already—and many more will die. Consider that before you lament how short this war may be."

Charley nodded.

"Sorry, Father," he said.

"It's alright, Charley. I do understand. Run along and prepare for dinner now."

Charley did as his father asked, pausing only to look over his shoulder as the door closed behind him. As he did, he could see his father fall into his mother's arms. He had never seen him look so distraught.

CHAPTER 3

Bull Run

Charley sat on the front porch of his parents' house, resting in the shade from the intense July heat. August was nearing and little had changed in the world around him. With school out for the summer, there was barely any talk about the goings on in the war. He knew that the Southerners were on the move. Mr. Lincoln, too, had been preparing. Charley could not guess when the first real battle might come, but he was soon to find out.

He watched the slow Sunday traffic moving down the street. Mostly older folks still in their church clothes and a bare few carriages passing by. It was a quiet summer day in West Chester, Pennsylvania. Then, the front door opened, and Pennell King stepped out.

Charley turned to see his father, his face pale as a ghost. He immediately jumped to his feet.

"What is it, Father?" he asked. "Is everything alright?"

"Mr. Gardener just stopped by while I was out back," Pennell explained. "He was just down the telegraph office. It's... well, there's no paper Sunday so we'll know more tomorrow, but... General McDowell engaged the Rebels at Bull Run in Virginia two days ago. The two armies fought from early morning into the evening until..."

Pennell shook his head and sighed.

"McDowell ordered the retreat at five pm. The Rebels took the day."

Charley's eyes grew wide, and he shook his head.

"But... what does that mean? We lost?"

"It means we lost," his father confirmed. "It means that the Rebels won a battle a stone's throw from Washington and Mr. Lincoln's army is on its heels. And I think it means this war is going to be longer than we all thought."

"What will you do?" Charley asked.

Pennell raised his head and looked Charley dead in the eye.

"More troops are being mustered as we speak," Pennell replied.

Charley nodded as his father continued.

"Things are about to get very different from what we're used to, Charley. I'm not certain if there will be a draft or something like it, but we'll know that soon enough. If I go, you may need to find work instead of going back to school this fall. I'm sorry."

"I understand, Father," Charley replied. "Wouldn't it... well, if the army pays maybe I should, um..."

"Charley," Pennell cut in, "I can't have this conversation again now. You can deliver papers, work in the mill, help with a harvest, or anything of that sort, but I can't risk sending you to war. It simply isn't safe."

Charley cast his eyes down to the ground but nodded in surrender.

"Have you talked to Mother about this, yet?" he asked.

Pennell sighed.

"She wore a brave face when I told her what was on my mind," Pennell said, "but I know she is feeling great stress. The thought of her staying here without me gives me greater pause than every musket and cannon in the Rebel Army. To be caught between a nation and a family is no trivial thing."

Charley frowned. He did not know how to comfort his father, but in his heart he felt his own torment. If the nation he loved was going to war, how could he not do his part? How could his father who raised him not see that same feeling in him?

He tried not to allow anger to overtake him, but the stubbornness of his parents frustrated him greatly. And if his father was so uncertain about going to war, why not stay and send Charley in his stead?

All these things raced through his head, but he could not bring himself to voice them. He knew it would only raise his father's ire. Instead, he simply stayed silent, which his father took as resignation.

"Why don't you run along with your drum now," Pennell said. "I have a few things to take care of and you should enjoy this summer the best you can."

Charley nodded and ran inside to grab his drum. As he did, he could hear his mother in the other room. She was crying softly. Charley wondered for a moment if he ought to try and comfort her, as he would have to in days to come, but he thought better of it.

"Father is still here," he whispered to himself. "And when Mother hears my drum, it will remind her that I'm not going anywhere."

The thought still pained him a bit, but he was resigned to the truth of it. He headed out onto the porch where his father was still standing. Pennell looked down at his son and sighed.

"Be good, Charley. And be strong."

Charley nodded and headed off down the street. When he was halfway down the block, he brought himself to attention and began to mark time. In a matter of moments, his mind was entirely focused on the rhythm. He began to move his feet along with the sound of his drum strikes. Closing his eyes, he could hear them echoing off the houses on either side of the street and did his best to tune out the errant sounds. Only the initial strikes mattered. On the battlefield, there were no buildings to cause echo. Only the clear, clean rapping of his snare.

Drumming out the order to march, Charley stepped forward at an even pace, making certain his tempo remained unchanged. The timing of each strike was of vital importance to the soldiers he now envisioned marching by his side. As he reached the first intersection, he gave the order to wheel left and they followed. Marching on at an even pace, everything but the road ahead and the soldiers beside him fell away and he was alone in the world. No passersby, no homes, and no horse carts to impede the progress of his company.

He must have cut an odd sight on that day, marching alone without his usual corps of children, and ignoring every person he passed. But he cared little about how he looked to others. On his mind were the battles he would not get the chance to see, the soldiers he would never get the chance to guide, and the nation he loved so much that he could do nothing to help defend.

Nothing.

Charley gritted his teeth and brought the sticks down all the harder on his drumhead. The sound blasted out in all directions as he struck his drum with a steady influx of frustration, never losing the beat, but growing in intensity with each passing moment.

Soon, the people he passed began to notice something was different about the boy who drummed all over town. Their concerned faces watched after him, but they might as well have been invisible. In his mind, they were bushes, rocks, trees, and other meaningless objects one passes while marching through the fields to battle. If they would not march beside him, they did not matter.

Alone now, even in his imagination, Charley marched toward where he knew the enemy lines would lie. Once the orders came, he would sound the charge. Ahead of him, the company captain was atop his horse, beckoning the men on. The time had come. The charge was ordered. Charley rapidly increased his rhythm and began to lurch forward at greater speed, following the captain until the man wheeled around on his horse and looked Charley dead in the eye.

He lurched to a stop, dropping his sticks as the world rushed back to him. The horse skittered back a step and whinnied. It was real, and so was the army captain atop it.

"Woah there," the captain said. "That was quite a charge to spook a war horse. What battle are you headed toward, boy?"

"My apologies, sir," Charley replied. "I suppose I wasn't paying attention to where I was going. I did not mean to surprise you so."

"I'm not certain surprise is the right word," the captain said. "I could hear you playing quite clearly, I believe since you first started. But don't you recognize me, Charley? I haven't been gone that long, have I?"

Charley looked up at the man for a few moments before he realized. The uniform, perhaps, confused him, but he knew the face well.

"Mr. Sweney," he said, "I did not know you were in town. I thought that you were at war."

"It's Captain Sweney these days," he said. "And I was, but I've been given a new task. How are you liking your new drum? I see it arrived in good condition. I must say I was surprised when I received your father's request, but I'm quite impressed to see how well you play it. I don't think there's another man in the army who could do better."

"It was you my father asked to send the drum?" Charley said. "Thank you so much, captain. It's wonderful."

"Good, I'm glad. Anyway, I'm just in town now and was going to head to the house in a bit. How is your father doing?"

"Well, I suppose," Charley said. "That is, he was doing quite well until news came of the battle in Virginia."

"That was a sad state of affairs," Capt. Sweney replied. "I suppose victory can never be assured. So tell me, Charley, how long have you been drumming?"

"Forever, I guess," Charley shrugged. "I don't really remember a time when I wasn't playing in some way. I just like keeping time, I suppose."

"Well, you are skilled at it. I have a deep love of music and I greatly appreciate a kindred spirit."

Charley forced a smile.

"Thank you… sir, would you mind if I asked you a question?"

"Go ahead."

"Well, if you're a captain in the army, what are you doing in West Chester? Shouldn't you be with your regiment?"

"Well," Capt. Sweney replied, "I suppose I should, but at the moment I don't have one. I'm here because Mr. Lincoln is looking for 300,000 men for three years of service. I'm to be captain of Company F in the 49th Pennsylvania Volunteers, but as of now the 49th regiment doesn't exist. It will soon, though."

"I see," Charley said. "Maybe my father will be in your company."

Though he tried not let on that he was upset, it was clear Capt. Sweney could sense something was bothering him. The captain swung down from his horse and looked Charley in the eye.

"Is something wrong, son? Are you worried about your father?"

"No," Charley said. "I'm… well, why did you decide to go to war, sir?"

Captain Sweney seemed taken aback by the question, but he took a moment to think it over before answering.

"I suppose I thought it was the right thing to do," he said. "I love this country and I want to fight for it. As far as I'm concerned, it is as simple as that."

Charley sighed.

"I wish my father saw it that way," he said.

"I don't understand," Captain Sweney replied. "I thought you said your father was going to enlist and fight?"

"Oh, he sees it that way when it comes to his own duty, should his country need him," Charley explained, "just not when it comes to me. I love this country, too, but I cannot go fight. I cannot even carry a drum."

Captain Sweney frowned.

"It sounds as if he wants to keep you safe. I don't believe there is anything wrong with a father thinking that way."

"Of course," Charley replied. "I understand that, I just... sorry, sir. I don't mean to be rude."

"Not at all. Listen, your father wants you to be safe, and I understand that. My father wants me and my brother John to be safe, too, no matter how old we've gotten. Much like your father, he would rather he be the one to fight while John and I stay safe at home.

"But I also understand your deep desire to come to the aid of your country. So... well, I can make no promises, Charley, but I *will* be the head of a company... and a company needs a drummer. Perhaps I can speak with your father."

Charley tried to contain his excitement. He knew his father was serious about keeping him safe and he had no chance of changing his mind on his own. But maybe with the help of a captain in the army, Pennell might just see things differently.

"You would do that for me?" Charley said. "What if he doesn't change his mind?"

"It cannot hurt to try," Captain Sweney replied. "I'll come by tomorrow morning and speak to him."

"Thank you so much, Captain Sweney. I will see you in the morning."

Captain Sweney nodded and Charley hurried off. For the first time in weeks, he traveled through town without drumming, determined to get home as quickly as possible. He wanted to tell his father he had met the captain, and he would be coming by in the morning. He thought it best not to say why, but his father did not care for surprise visitors, so he would be wise to tell him.

When he arrived home, however, his father was nowhere to be found. His mother sat in the kitchen, waiting for a pot of water to boil. She smiled when she saw him, but there was a sadness in her eyes.

"W…where's Father?" he asked.

"Oh, still at the shop," his mother replied in a pensive tone. "An order came in last night for uniforms to outfit a new regiment. Your father thinks there's a chance he can hold off joining up if he's providing a much-needed service for the troops. And the money will be good for whenever he is called upon to join."

"Oh," Charley said, surprised at his father's change of fortune. "But…"

Charley paused, uncertain how to explain what had happened. It occurred to him as he stood there, though, that if his father was not ready to enlist and Captain Sweney had only just begun to build his company, that he and his father might not find themselves together when the time came to muster.

"He doesn't want to go?" Charley asked. His mother looked back at him, puzzled.

"What do you mean?"

"I just mean, is he trying to avoid going to war?" Charley clarified. "I thought he felt… and then the captain was going to… I'm not…"

"The captain? Charley, you're not making much sense, dear. What are you trying to say? This is *good* news. I know how much you believe in the cause, but this way your father can help the effort without being in danger."

"It's not that, it's just… while I was drumming today, I ran into Captain Sweney, from next door. He said I was doing a very good job and… well, he said he was helping to muster a new regiment and needed a drummer for his company…"

His mother's face twisted into shock.

"Sweney? Benjamin Sweney told you he needed a drummer for his company?"

Charley could not tell if his mother was angry, disappointed, sad, or all three in a manner that only a mother could be. He timidly nodded his head and waited for her to continue.

"And I suppose he intends to convince your father that this drummer should be you, is that the case?"

Charley nodded.

"Oh Charley," she said, exasperated, "what am I to do with you? You are so eager to go out to war and leave me here alone."

"But that's not what it's about, Mother," Charley pleaded. "It's about standing up for something, right? Don't you believe that the Union needs to stay together? After today, there's no way to be sure it will—unless everyone who can lend a hand does."

"Perhaps I question what good a nation will do me if I do not have my family," his mother replied. Charley did not know what to say and, after a moment his mother sighed and shook her head.

"In the end, it doesn't matter what I think. You will grow and someday go on your way. When Benjamin comes, he'll talk to your father. Whatever your father decides will be what happens. I just want you to promise me one thing, Charley."

"Anything, Mother."

"If you go," she said, "or I suppose when you go… you may spend every hour among men from all over this nation but remember one thing—you are my boy. You will be my boy when you march away, my boy when you go into battle, my boy when you come home, and even if you should grow tall as a mighty oak you will still be my boy. Do you understand?"

Charley was surprised to find a tear threatening to fall from his eye. Something in his mother's words moved him so, that for a moment, he regretted the very thought of going to war. But the moment passed, and he found himself filled with great resolve.

"I understand, Mother," he said. "And I hope to always make you proud of your boy."

"I am," his mother replied. "Run along now, Charley. Dinner will be ready soon enough."

★ ★ ★

The rest of that day passed with little event, and Charley met the next morning at dawn, too excited to remain in his bed. By the time the sun had risen fully over the houses of West Chester, he was waiting by the window for the captain to arrive. His father came downstairs half an hour later and saw him huddled by the window in great anticipation. He shook his head, but said nothing, knowing that the time to speak on the matter would come soon enough. Instead, he went into the kitchen to find the morning paper Charley had brought in earlier.

They did not have to wait long at all before Captain Sweney appeared on the block, making his way toward the Kings' home. He was still in his uniform, riding his horse toward them. He stopped and tied the beast to the porch before walking to the door and knocking. Charley moved to answer it, but his father gestured for him to sit back down and wait. A moment later, Captain Sweney was inside.

"I've not seen you for some time, Benjamin," his father said. "You've done quite well for yourself, I see."

"As have you, Pennell," Capt. Sweney replied. "You have a fine home. It almost makes a man jealous to see such a fine picture of domestic life. A military tent is of little comfort."

"Indeed," Pennell said. "You, of course, know my son, Charley. The other children are still upstairs, and my wife Adaline is in the kitchen. Would you like to come sit down and have breakfast?"

"That is very kind of you, Pennell. I'll accept. Do you have any coffee?"

"I am certain we can brew some up for you," Pennell replied.

The two men walked into the kitchen where further pleasantries were exchanged with Charley's mother. Once they were seated, Charley moved closer so he could hear the conversation that followed.

"So," his father said, "I understand you've spoken to my boy about being a drummer for your company."

"Yes, Mr. King. I apologize if I overstepped my boundaries. The boy nearly crashed into me while I was riding through town, and I happened to notice his considerable skill with the instrument."

"Call me Pennell, Benjamin. We are not strangers. Would you prefer I call you captain, though?"

"Not at all. Ben is just fine."

"Very well, Ben," Pennell replied. "I understand your company is to be part of the 49th Pennsylvania, organizing in September. Is that correct?"

"It is," Capt. Sweney said. "Before you give me your thoughts on the matter of Charley's joining, I do want to say that I am very understanding of your feelings on the matter. This is no small thing to be undertaken lightly. War is a dangerous proposition, for all involved. That said, precision is paramount when moving and positioning troops, and I have heard your son play. I venture to say he understands the importance of precision."

"In music, certainly," Pennell allowed, "but the streets of West Chester are not the fields of Virginia, Ben. And cannonballs do not discriminate between musket and drum."

"That is true, but your boy will not be in the thick of it. When battle commences, he would be behind the company. I will make sure of that. He will stay safe."

"How can you promise that?" Charley heard his mother ask. "You have no control over what the other side will do. The Rebels will fire upon anyone in blue. They have no regard for age."

"I will see to it myself," Captain Sweney replied. "As long as I stand—as long as I hold my command—I promise to ensure your son's safety. He will not be hurt under my watch."

"What about your brother, John?" Pennell said. "I have heard that he is forming a regimental band in Delaware. Perhaps Charley could join him? I would think a musician of his caliber would be leading reviews, parades, and such."

"I'm afraid even John will likely be pulled into the conflict," Captain Sweney answered. "This war, it appears, will be much greater than any of us thought. We may need every able-bodied man in the nation to fight and John is just that, regardless of his musical prowess. The war, it seems, is coming for us all."

Charley heard his father sigh, and he knew the man was deep in thought. He found himself thinking back to what his mother said the day before, that whatever his father decided would be final. His future balanced on the brink as he held his breath through the silence. Finally, after nearly a minute, his father spoke.

"You'll make it part of your duty to protect him?" his father asked. "You give me your word?"

"On my honor," Captain Sweney said, "he will not come to harm."

Charley let out a long breath. They rose to their feet and walked out of the kitchen to where Charley was waiting. Behind them, he could see his mother standing with a hand over her mouth. The look on her face pained him deeply, but nothing could turn him back now.

"Well," the captain said, "I suppose you could hear all that from here. Enjoy the rest of your summer, Charley. Come September, we muster."

CHAPTER 4

Goodbyes

As the sun rose on that early September morning, Charley, for the first time, felt apprehensive. It was hard to overstate his excitement in the days leading up to the official muster of the 49th Pennsylvania Volunteers. He could barely sleep ever since the calendar turned to September and, quite frankly, he'd not slept well all summer. Most nights, he sat up drumming on the bed for hours after he was expected to be asleep. At first, his father would scold him for not getting his rest, but after a while he gave up and asked that Charley simply keep the noise to a minimum.

Soon, though, it would be his duty to wake others with his drumming. That, his father often said, was one of the many talents necessary for a Drum Major that Charley already possessed. He was also already well versed in waking up before the dawn, though as his father reminded him, rarely had he marched ten miles the day before waking up so early. Still, Charley had never been one to crave long hours of sleep, especially not when there was important work—or drumming—to be done.

That particular morning, the task of the coming day was muster. In a matter of hours, he would form up with Company F of the 49th Pennsylvania Volunteer Infantry and head off toward Harrisburg to join the rest of the division. Then, they would march south to join the Army of the Potomac and prepare for the next campaign.

Little in the way of major battles had occurred since the embarrassment at Bull Run. The North set about growing its strength while the South prepared for invasion. Charley drummed and marched and attended school when it was called back into session. He was not certain why he should go, but there seemed no question in his mother's mind that it was necessary. There would be no school today, though. And not for many days to come.

On a different day, that thought might be exciting. Today, however, it was more sobering than anything else. There was a lot ahead of Charley and none of it was anything he'd experienced before. Everything would be new but for one thing—his drum.

Rising to his feet, Charley crossed the room and picked up that drum, strapping it over his shoulder. His bag was already packed with the bare few belongings he chose to bring and he threw that over his other arm, then headed down the stairs. When he reached the living room, he found his younger brother sitting by the window, using the early morning light to mend a pair of trousers. Lewis was talented in that regard and often did small jobs for his friends, who in turn paid him with small coins, old toys, or other trinkets. He would do it for free though, Charley knew. Lewis was so much like their father in that regard. He simply loved the work.

As he walked into the room, Lewis heard him and looked up.

"Charley," he said, "I was worried I might miss you."

"Miss me?" Charley replied. "It's barely past dawn. Did you think I would be leaving overnight? You didn't have to get up so early."

Lewis shifted a bit in his chair and looked at the floor.

"I never exactly fell asleep," he confessed. "I suppose I was thinking about you going off to war all night. I suppose I was worried."

Charley frowned.

"Worried about what? Father's not going off to war, at least not yet. And mother still has him *and* you to watch over her. What's there to worry about?"

"Well, you of course," Lewis said. "How could any of us not be worried about you? You're gone off to war and there's nothin' we can do."

"I'm going to be fine, Lewis," Charley insisted. "I'm the drummer boy. No one is going to try to hurt the drummer boy."

"I guess you're right," Lewis said. "Do you think you'll stay just the drummer boy? If the war goes on, will you start fighting?"

"I don't know," Charley confessed. "Captain Sweney says he's only got one other soldier under nineteen in the company, and he's a musician, too. That would mean the war would have to go on for seven more years and most folks didn't think it would go on as long as it has as is."

"But they were wrong," Lewis replied.

"Yeah, well… I guess we'll just have to see. Anyway, I've only enlisted for a three-year term, so even if the war continues, I'd have to reenlist to fight longer."

"I would be thirteen by then," Lewis said, pursing his lips. "Maybe I should start learning the drum so I can take your place and you can stay home."

Charley smiled.

"Or you can learn the fife or bugle, and we can march together."

"Maybe," Lewis said.

"Let's not make any such plans just yet," their father put in, appearing in the archway leading in from the hall. "No need to send the whole King family rushing down to Virginia."

"Are you sure?" Charley said. "Mom wouldn't have to worry about missing me if we all joined up."

Pennell allowed a humorless chuckle.

"I suppose levity is appropriate for moments like this, but I can't seem to take any pleasure in it."

The boys looked at each other, confused, but their father waved it off.

"There's much to do today, boys. I'm afraid I'm a bit preoccupied with what's to come. And, of course, there will be no respite when Charley marches off. I've orders backing up to fill my next two weeks. I suppose it's well to keep busy."

"In that case," Lewis said, "I'd be happy to help out around the shop—when school is out, of course."

"I may take you up on that offer," Pennell replied. "An extra set of capable hands is likely to be required."

Charley smiled at the exchange. It was comforting in a way to see that things would continue while he was gone, and that his family would pull together as they always had when he was around. Lewis would do well in the shop, and he already did quite well in school. Their parents were already quite proud of him, and Charley was certain the coming months would only increase that pride. He knew they were proud of him for what he was doing, but there was a sadness in that pride. Lewis, he was certain, would bring them nothing but joy.

His mother appeared as he considered this and that very sense was immediately apparent on her face. She crossed the room quickly and took him in her arms. Charley let his bag and drum slip slowly to the floor and then hugged his mother. A moment later, Lewis had joined the hug and his father was standing near, too, his hand on Adaline's shoulder. Many moments passed before a word was spoken between them and, when she spoke, Charley's mother could barely muster more than a whisper.

"I love you, Charley," she said. "I'm... proud... and I love you."

Tears sprang unwillingly to Charley's eyes as he smiled at his mother. Her face, too, was soaked, though she smiled through the sadness.

"I love you, too, Mother."

There was nothing more to say. Charley reached down and picked up his things. His father patted him on the shoulder and they walked out the door down to the street. When they reached the street, Charley glanced back at the house. Lewis and his mother stood at the door, and he gave them his best smile. Lewis answered with a weak wave and his mother just watched on through her tears. Charley looked up at his father, who only nodded and nodded.

It was time to leave West Chester behind. It was time to march to war.

CHAPTER 5

Muster

October 1, 1861
One Mile Northeast of Lewinsville, VA

Charley's feet hurt. The past week and a half had been a blur. The 49th Pennsylvania had mustered in the capital, Harrisburg, and been attached to the Fourth Corps of the Army of the Potomac. Captain Benjamin Sweney's command, Company F, was comprised of about 150 men and ten or so officers. Their time in Harrisburg seemed rather brief to him, though it must have been two weeks. They were met shortly after their arrival by Governor Curtin, after whom their encampment was named.

The governor gave a fine speech, though Charley could not say he remembered much of it. What he remembered most were the fine colors Governor Curtin presented them with—flags of both the state and nation. The sight of them made Charley proud to stand in uniform with the others around him.

When Governor Curtin was finished, the commander of the Regiment, Colonel William Irwin, got up to speak. He had an ill-kempt beard and slicked-back hair that nearly reached his collar, and while he cut an impressive figure in uniform, something about him reminded Charley of the older fellow who always stood around by the public house in the center of town. Charley would later learn that Irwin was a veteran of the Mexican War, which could have accounted for the similarities he saw, as the old man from West Chester had fought in that conflict as well.

When the colonel spoke, his voice was deep and carried with it a distinctively cluttered characteristic. His speech was impassioned and deeply patriotic, though some of his words ran together now and then. In it, he implored them all to fight bravely. At the end of the speech, he turned to the fine regimental colors presented to them and said,

"Boys, while I have an arm to wield a sword or a man to fire a gun, these colors should never drop in the face of the enemy—nor be desecrated by the touch of rebel hands. I vow here and now that this will not happen. Will you join me in this vow?"

The regiment roared back in agreement and the ceremony came to an end.

Charley's portrait as it appears in the State Museum of Pennsylvania. When and how the image was restored remains undocumented. (Robert S. Westbrook, *History of the 49th Pennsylvania Volunteers* (Altoona, PA: Altoona Time Print, 1898))

Perhaps a week later, they left Harrisburg by train, crossing through Maryland with stops at Baltimore and the Capital, before crossing the Potomac into Virginia. At the end of September, they finally made camp outside Lewinsville. Even though they had long stretches of train rides, the marches in between were exhausting. Charley did his best to keep up as they traveled, though each night he found himself more tired than the day before. When they finally made camp, he felt like he been walking for his entire life.

As he began to prepare his bunk, Charley found himself being approached by another boy, older than him but far younger than most others in the army. He stood up and noticed that in the side of the boy's pack was a fife.

"You're the other musician, then?" Charley said.

"Yep, I met up with the column after the march started," the boy replied. "The name is Joseph Keene, from Moscow. You can call me Joe."

Joe reached out his hand, and Charley accepted it willingly.

"Charley King," he said, "from West Chester."

"Same town as the captain," Joe said. "Did you know him?"

"His family lives near mine," Charley explained. "Do you mind if I ask you how old you are? I don't mean to be rude, but you seem younger than the rest. And well, obviously I am, too."

"I'm sixteen," Joe replied. "About as young as they let you in, although… you seem a good bit younger."

"Twelve," Charley said, sheepishly. "I was allowed in by special request of Captain Sweney on account of he heard me drumming and thought I was good. He promised my father he'd keep an eye on me and make sure I'm safe."

Joe chuckled.

"What's so funny?" Charley asked, feeling the hairs on his neck bristle. Joe seemed surprised to see him become upset so quickly.

"Didn't mean anything by it," Joe said. "I was just thinkin' my Mother woulda liked a promise like that. Not sure how anyone can honestly say that once it comes to battle. Was nice of him, though."

"Yeah…"

"So, you're the drummer?" Joe said, after a short pause. "How long have you been playing?"

"Long as I can remember," Charley replied. "How long have you been on fife?"

"Just a few months, actually," Joe said. "I suppose I'm a fast learner, though. I've got a few songs I know, and most o' the orders and what not. You know any songs?"

"A couple. I mostly learned the field orders and all that, but yeah. I know a few."

Joe pulled out his fife and smiled.

"You know 'Froggy in the Well?'"

"Sure," Charley chuckled. He strapped on his drum and then beat out a few notes to make sure it was in order. Then, with a nod, he launched into the song. Joe played along, only struggling a bit on the first chorus. A few of the other soldiers stopped and watched as they played, smiles creeping onto their faces. One or two of the younger men began a jaunty sort of dance and the rest began to laugh. Charley smiled, keeping an even tempo through the song as Joe did his best to play along.

When they had finished, the soldiers around them began to clap, and Charley felt a mixture of pride and nervousness. Joe saw his face turning red and clapped him on the shoulder.

"We'll have to do more of that," he said. "Looks like the men liked it."

As he said that, three of the soldiers walked over to them smiling. They were young and fresh-faced, though not as young as Joe and Charley. One of them, a dark-haired, blue-eyed man of about twenty, reached out his hand to shake. Charley accepted the greeting with a smile.

"Alfred Moulder," the man said, "out of West Chester. There's something familiar about you."

"I'm Charley King. I'm from West Chester, too. You may have seen—or more likely heard—me playing around town over the past few months."

"Right, the little drummer boy," Alfred replied. "I didn't know you were old enough to enlist. No offense meant, of course, I just thought you were closer to my nephew's age. He's nine."

"I'm twelve," Charley said, pausing for a moment before adding, "and a half."

Alfred nodded.

"Good to know. I understand Captain Sweney made a special exception for you?"

"Yes, he's a friend of the family," Charley replied.

"And what a family those Sweneys are," Alfred said with a laugh. "That John might be the best musician I've ever heard of. I understand Benjamin... erm, the captain, is quite talented himself."

"He is certainly a music lover, to say the least," Charley agreed.

"So what's your name, fife player?" Alfred asked.

"Joseph Keene from Moscow, PA. You can call me Joe."

"Well, isn't that funny," Alfred said. "That nine-year-old nephew of mine is named Joseph. Doesn't that just tickle ya? Anyway, this here is Chuck Butler from Unionville, and my buddy Lenny Appleman."

"Good to meet you both," Chuck said. "I do love a good tune. Wish I had learned to play a little something, but I never found the time. Lenny here's got a banjo. I can't imagine why he wants to add any extra weight to these packs, though."

"You'll get it when we all play together," Lenny said with a chuckle. "Nothing completes a song like the banjo."

"Good to know," Alfred put in. "It's good to..."

Alfred cut off mid-sentence and snapped to attention. The rest followed suit. Charley whirled around to find Captain Sweney standing behind him. He saluted, bringing his feet together tight.

"Sound the assembly, Mr. King," he said. "The rest of you lot fall in."

Without a moment's pause, Charley raised his sticks and began to beat out "The Assembly." The others, with Joe being the exception, hurried to fall into ranks. The rest of Company F followed suit, making perfect lines in front of Captain Sweney as he watched. He nodded, a small smile creeping into the corners of his mouth, as the last few fell in.

Once all were assembled, he nodded to Charley, who cut off the cadence. Turning to the troops, he raised his chin proudly.

"Welcome to Lewinsville, men of Company F. I know the last few days have been grueling and, to many of you may seem like a blur, but Colonel Irwin thought it wise to move quickly and join the rest of our corps. The 49th Regiment has been attached to the brigade of Winfield Scott Hancock, newly minted general on this very day.

"That means we are under the command of Brigadier General W. F. Smith, himself a veteran of the battle of Bull Run, and part of the Fourth Corps under Major General William B. Franklin. Above him stands

General George McClellan, Commander of the Army of the Potomac who reports to President Abraham Lincoln, who himself reports to God and the people of these United States.

"But with the possible exception of Col. Irwin and the Almighty Himself, I do not expect you to meet or converse with any of these individuals. Assembled to my right and left are the men from which you will receive your orders. These are the men you will go to with questions and the men who will have all the answers that you need. If they do not have the answer, you do not need the answer. Is that understood?"

"Yes, sir," the company replied in chorus. Captain Sweney nodded, keeping his stiff and serious appearance. His look was so different from the day Charley met him in West Chester that he wondered for a moment if it was the same man at all. But, after a few seconds had passed, Captain Sweney smiled, and the man Charley knew reappeared.

"Good," he said. "I'm glad to have such a fine company."

Sweney gestured to a short, meek-looking man directly beside him and continued.

"To my right is Lt. Wombacker. He is my second in command. Any order you receive from him might as well be an order directly from myself. To his right is Sgt. Philip Haines. Any order you receive from him might as well be an order directly from Lt. Wombacker, and you know how to treat orders from Lt. Wombacker."

A light, uneasy laugh trickled through the crowd. Sweney waited for it to fade before continuing.

"To my left is the best friend you will have in this army, Lt. John Gray, our Quartermaster. Anything you need, Lt. Gray will be able to get it for you. If Lt. Gray cannot get it for you, that means you do not need it. Understood?"

"Yes, sir!"

"Good, now to the left of your best friend in this army is your worst enemy in this army, Sgt. Don Juan Wallings. For those of you who can read and have sought out culture in your readings, do not let Sgt. Wallings' name fool you. He is no romantic and the only thing he loves is drilling volunteers until they are flawless, eminently skilled, and unflinchingly brave professional soldiers. That is what you will be by the time the coming winter is over.

"This army was caught off-guard by the well-prepared and determined soldiers of the Rebel Army. They embarrassed us on the field of battle and sent our army retreating back to Washington. They embarrassed our people, our families and friends, as well as everything a northerner stands for. Worst of all, they embarrassed Mr. Lincoln—and that will not stand.

"So men, as the leaves begin to fall, you will drill and train. When snow covers the ground, you will train and drill. For Christmas, you will be receiving training. Anyone with birthdays, your gift will be training. When the snow begins to melt, you will drill and train.

"And when the winter clears and the ground begins to thaw, you will be the finest outfit of soldiers ever to grace this land. This is your *only* goal from now until we march. This is why you will wake. This is why you will eat. This is why you will sleep. For no other reason than to prepare to embarrass Johnny Reb in return for our own embarrassment, and send him back to Richmond with his tail between his legs.

"Do you men understand?"

"Yes, sir," came the chorus.

"Good," Captain Sweney said, "then I guess you'd better get training. Mr. King!"

With an audible snap, Charley raised his sticks into position.

"Sound the Tattoo," Sweney continued. "It's time for evening drills. Sgt. Wallings, command is yours."

Charley began the cadence as Captain Sweney led Lt. Wombacker, Sgt. Haines, and Lt. Gray back to his tent. Sgt. Wallings stepped forward, looking down his nose at the troops standing at attention. He made a great show of frowning at their posture and instructed one soldier to raise his shoulders by rapping him on the arm with a baton. Once the first soldier had been corrected, the rest of the company followed suit, which brought a smile to the sergeant's face.

"Good," he said, as Charley finished the Tattoo. "I like men who are willing to be corrected. For the next several months, the most productive things you can do are listen and work hard. If you do both those things, you'll find a place in this army. Now, it'll take some time to get everything straight. There are many orders and you will not only need to know how to execute them, but how to recognize them in the heat of battle.

"For that, we use the drum and, if we have one, the bugle. You'll notice we don't have a bugle, so it'll be the drum. Once our young drummer boy has learned *all* his drum calls… which may take some time judging by his age, we'll have to learn those fast."

Charley pursed his lips at the sergeant's remark, which seemed rather pointed and insulting. What's more, it was terribly inaccurate. Charley had gotten his hands on the latest military drum, fife, and bugle manual the moment his father had allowed him to enlist. He spent the rest of the summer learning everything in the manual and now could play it all flawlessly. To suggest he knew nothing was upsetting, especially after he had just played the Tattoo perfectly.

As he stewed, he noticed Joe leaning over toward him.

"Don't worry too much about it," he whispered. "We'll learn it all together."

Charley rolled his eyes, but said nothing as Sgt. Wallings prepared to teach them the fundamentals of marching.

"Alright," Wallings said, "you're already at attention. That's good, but it's also real simple. The first thing you're going to have to learn is how to right face. Now…"

Pup-pa-rup!

Wallings turned to Charley and his eyes narrowed.

"Know that one, do you? And left face, too, I suppose?"

Pup. Pup-pa-rup!

"Reveille? Forward march? Wheel left? Wheel right? Come prepared did we?"

Charley executed each cadence perfectly, keeping his eyes locked ahead so as not to lose his concentration. Sgt. Wallings watched as he played, his stare never leaving his face. Charley could practically feel the sergeant's glare boring into his body, but he kept on regardless. He did not know what would happen when he finished, so he kept on playing each requested call.

When, at last, Wallings ran out of calls to order, the field fell silent. Charley passed the left stick into his right hand, and then slammed both arms to his side. Out of the corner of his eye, he could see Wallings standing frozen and wondered if he was angry… or something worse.

After a few moments, the sergeant walked up to Charley, stopping just a few feet from him.

"You know 'The Minstrel Boy'?" he asked.

"Yes sir," Charley replied.

"Good, it's one of my favorite songs to march to. Fall in."

Charley hurried over and fell in line with the rest of the troops. Wallings then turned to Joe, who stood frozen a few feet away.

"I don't suppose you know the whole drill book as well, Keene?"

"Not... um, not quite, sir," Joe replied. "I could maybe use a day or two to get it all straight, if you don't mind, sir."

"Go practice," he said, turning away. "It seems Mr. King will be staying here with us... to drill."

CHAPTER 6

Drill and Train

Sgt. Wallings was as good as his word. The company, and indeed the entire regiment, spent all day everyday drilling and training. At first, Charley thought he would not make it through the first week. As much time as he spent marching and drumming back in West Chester, nothing could compare to this. His already calloused hands were rubbed to the point of bleeding several times and his legs often buckled under him as he marched.

But as time passed, he realized he was growing stronger. His legs felt sturdier at the end of the day and his hands had grown so rough that he thought not even a musket ball could break the skin. It was hard living, but he grew more and more accustomed to it day by day.

Most days were like every other day in Camp Griffin. One exception was the afternoon of November 20. They had started out from camp early in the morning to attend a review at Munson's Hill just outside of Arlington, VA. They arrived around ten o'clock and waited until noon when General McClellan and his staff arrived. This in itself would have been a very special occurrence, but on that particular day, Gen. McClellan had brought along another well-respected leader:

President Abraham Lincoln.

Charley had been nervous enough before he learned of the president's arrival, but now he could barely keep his hands still. The 49th was near the front when the review began, and Charley could see Mr. Lincoln standing among the army brass. It was not difficult to pick him out from the crowd. He was one of the few wearing civilian clothes, true, but he was also a head taller than anyone else around him.

None could miss their great commander-in-chief, but Charley could only get a quick look in now and then. He had been told in no uncertain terms by Sgt. Wallings that he was to keep his eyes front as they marched. He and his comrades were not to break stride or look about. Only the captain and higher officers were allowed to salute the dais. When they discussed this earlier, Joe said he would cautiously sneak a look when he had a chance, but it seemed as though Wallings had heard of this plan. He marched right next to the two of them and though he too did not break his gaze, Charley had the strange feeling that he was watching them the entire time.

As it turned out, however, seeing President Lincoln was not the most exciting thing to happen to the 49th that day. Once the regiment had passed the dais and much to the surprise of Charley, Wallings, and likely all 70,000 troops in attendance, Col. Irwin called out the order to wheel right. Unwilling to disobey the order, Capt. Sweney echoed, as did the other company leaders, and the entire regiment turned off the road. Only a few moments later, Irwin called for the company to halt.

"What in the damned hell…" Charley had heard Wallings mutter, but there was little time to say much else. Col. Irwin began to shout out drill orders. Charley saw Capt. Sweney look to one of his fellow captains, but the man just frowned and shook his head. A moment later, they both echoed the orders. Charley and the other drummers followed without hesitation and the regiment began their drills.

Behind them, the other regiments were forced to come to a halt and the review began to back up. Charley chanced a look toward the road behind them and he could see the that the parade was in disarray. Amid the chaos, a general on horseback came riding forward, his face red with anger. He shouted so loudly that Charley could hear him over the din of his snare drum.

"What is the meaning of this, Colonel?"

Irwin wheeled his horse around, so flustered he nearly fell off.

"Drilling the regiment, sir," he replied. Irwin seemed confused by the question.

"In the middle of a damned parade?" Hancock shouted back. "Move your men along, double quick. And once you've gotten them out of the way, present yourself at the stockade! I do believe you are half-soused, colonel."

"The stock... sir? Who will lead the men?" Irwin asked.

"Give Major Hulings command and remove yourself double-quick!"

Irwin was hot, but he knew better than to contradict the general, particularly in front of McClellan, not to mention President Lincoln. He slunk off as Major Hulings rode his horse to the forefront and took over giving orders. They were back in proper form within a few minutes and the parade continued.

For his breach of discipline, Colonel Irwin was tried by court martial, but nothing much came of it. The excitement was short lived, and while Major Hulings was quite capable and ran a tight ship, things felt more normal when Colonel Irwin returned to command. But that was September and things had been rather dull since then.

It was October now and the air was cold and heavy. The early mornings were no trouble for Charley. He was a naturally early riser. The same could not be said for Joe, who rarely woke up without help. That morning, Charley had to shake Joe awake. He tried to roll away but found himself nearly falling off his bunk. He muttered as he sat upright and looked around. The hut was pitch dark and Charley could barely make out Joe's face, let alone anyone else inside.

"Come on, Joe. It's almost dawn and Sgt. Wallings hates a late Reveille. Get a move on."

"How am I supposed to play the blasted fife when I can't move my fingers? How is it so cold here? I thought we marched south."

"Hardly."

"This is Virginia, ain't it? South. It ain't supposed to snow in the South."

"Maybe in Georgia, but it's sure snowing in Virginia now. Maybe the state just doesn't want us here."

Joe chuckled, swinging his legs out from under his blanket.

"Well, that much we know is certain. Alright, I'm up. I'll be out in a few minutes, and we can ruin these boys' morning together."

Joe was as good as his word. He met Charley outside, and together they roused the troops. Once the camp began to stir, they took up positions by the flagpole and prepared for the colors. They stood, stomping their feet every few moments, and watching their own breath hang in the air in front of them. Joe played with his keys a little, most likely to make sure they were still working. Charley tucked his hands into his coat and waited for the others to arrive.

About ten minutes later, the color guard arrived with the flag, and Charley and Joe snapped to attention. They began to play "To the Colors" as the flag was attached to the pole and raised. Once the flag was up, the group dispersed, and Charley and Joe played "Peas on the Trench" to call the troops to breakfast.

When they were finished, they broke for the mess hall, hoping to get their food as quickly as possible. Many of their fellow soldiers had already arrived, so they had to wait for their porridge. It was a passable breakfast, not much different from what they might have at home. Sausage would have made a fine addition, but it was rare to experience such a pleasure in the mornings.

After breakfast, it was time for morning drill. Charley and Joe called the men to form up and come to attention. As with every morning, Captain Sweney came out to examine the troops. He rarely had much to tell them, as news of the goings-on in the South was few and far between. The winter had slowed everything and everyone in the nation, war or not. Both armies were largely waiting for the snow to melt and the ground to thaw for the conflict to resume. As such, morning reviews usually consisted of Captain Sweney encouraging his men to keep focused and work hard, then congratulating them on their progress so far.

Once Capt. Sweney was finished, Sgt. Wallings would take over and drills would continue as they did every morning. Nearly four months of training having passed, Company F had mastered most movements asked of them, but as Wallings was fond of reminding them, everything changes when the bullets begin to fly. He reminded them frequently that their drill would need to become so ingrained in their minds that they naturally moved as a unit without even thinking about it. It must become second nature.

To Charley, much of what he had to do already *was* second nature, to the point where he began to find it difficult to focus on the orders he received. It was easy enough to follow the other soldiers as they moved, but on long stretches of unbroken march, he found himself fiddling with the cadence, rather than playing the straight rhythms requested of him. He did not make drastic changes, of course, just few extra strikes now and then. Occasionally, he would strike the rim in place of the head, giving a noticeable change of tone to whatever marching tune he was playing.

For the most part, his improvisation went unnoticed by anyone other than Joe, who found it entertaining to hear Charley take liberties with the music. On the rare occasion that Wallings noticed, Charley would be met with a stark, narrow-eyed glare and he would snap back to the music as written. Nothing much came of these instances, though, until one particular afternoon when Wallings had dismissed the company for evening duties. He caught Charley by the arm as he was leaving, saying, "Wait just a moment there, Mr. King."

Charley felt his heart rate pick up as he turned to face the sergeant. "Yes, sir?" he said.

"Don't think I haven't noticed what you've been doing with the cadences—mixing up your patterns and what not. I've been lenient so far, but I need you to listen and take me seriously. I've said a dozen if not a hundred times how important it is to make certain our every move is like clock-work. Anything that might upset the movements of this unit will jeopardize its effectiveness and—believe me when I say that I am by no means exaggerating—hurt this army's chances of winning the war.

"Now, you're a fine drummer for your age, boy, but make no mis-take—you show that age when you fool with the prescribed cadences. Mr. Keene may find your behavior entertaining, but you will notice he has never once intentionally changed his presentation during our marches. With age comes wisdom. I suggest you age quickly in that regard. Do you understand?"

Charley could feel his face growing red as the sergeant spoke. Part of him wanted to be defiant in the face of the scolding, but most of him knew that the sergeant was right. He had begun to lose focus during the drills and that would not do when it came time to do battle. Still, he could not hold down the trembling that rose from his chest to his arms. Unable to speak, he nodded frantically.

Wallings frowned for a moment, but looked satisfied. With a nod, he turned around and headed off to his own duties. Once he was gone, Charley exhaled and tears followed. His evening duties consisted almost entirely of practicing, so he hurried back to his bunk. Dropping his drum beside the bed, he hopped in and pulled his sheet over his head. The tears would not stop and he was terrified the other soldiers would see him and ridicule him. In the bunk, however, he was safe from prying eyes.

For the first time since he left West Chester, he realized how much he missed home. He had never been away from his parents for more than a week, let alone four months. Lately, more than ever, he found himself thinking about home—marching around town where the faces were friendly and he knew his mother was waiting not far away. She had remarked before he left that she found it comforting when she could hear him drumming all over town. She never had to be concerned about where he was. In a way, Charley also found it comforting that she could always hear him. She wouldn't worry about losing him and he didn't have to worry about being lost. That was far from the case now.

Now, he had little idea what his mother was doing, or even exactly how far he was from her. If he were lost, would anyone notice? Would anybody wonder where the sounds of the drummer boy had gone?

His thoughts cut short at the sound of footsteps approaching. They passed his bunk, but paused and took two steps back toward him.

"Charley?" came a familiar voice. Charley peaked out from under his blanket to see Alfred Moulder standing by his bunk.

"Something wrong?" Alfred asked.

"N-no..."

"Uh huh," Alfred replied, clearly unconvinced. "Looks a little like something is wrong. Did Sgt. Wallings say something to upset you?"

"No," Charley said. "Well, yes but he was right. I can't fool around when it comes to war. I'll get someone killed."

"He said that?"

"Not exactly," Charley confessed, "but it's true. He was just telling me to be more serious, and I couldn't stop myself from getting upset. Can you imagine if some of the older soldiers had seen me with tears in my eyes? I can't believe I could be so... so weak."

"Charley," Alfred replied, donning his most comforting tone, "try to remember that as brave as you are for volunteering to play the drum with the army, you are still a twelve-year-old boy. I would say that one moment of breaking down is nothing to be ashamed of. Why, I often find myself wondering if this is truly my place, or if I should not have stayed home with my family. I grow wistful thinking of it and, to be quite honest, I've shed a tear or two. That, of course, is just between the two of us."

"Of course," Charley replied. "Really, though? You've cried at the thought of your family?"

"Sure," Alfred said. "My brother William is fighting as well, with the 1st Independence Battery, Company A, I believe. My parents were sad to see us go, but they won't want for company. I have quite a few siblings. I suppose it's me that needs company more than them. Luckily, I've got you, and Chuck, Lenny, and Joe. Good lot, don't you think?"

"Yeah," Charley answered, allowing a small smile.

"I'm glad you agree. Now, I've got to take care of my evening duties and you need to... well, I suppose you don't really *need* to practice, but it would go a long way to endear you to Sgt. Wallings if he heard you practicing."

"Everyone needs to practice," Charley replied.

"Good mindset," Alfred said. "Anyway, a few of us were going to gather around a fire tonight after supper. Lenny wants to break out the banjo and hopefully dispel some of the cold for a bit. The boys have been through the mill and we could use a little fun. A drum would help. And let Joe know he should come along."

"Sure thing," Charley replied. Alfred gave him a nod and then continued on with his business. Charley rose to his feet and strapped his drum back on his shoulder. Heading out of the bunk, he began to practice.

It was easy enough for Charley to fall back into the music, letting it overtake all other thoughts and become his sole focus. These days, cold and long as they were, his hands never grew tired. Back in West Chester, he couldn't imagine there was any way he could spend more time on his drum, but the camp near Lewinsville proved him quite wrong. He drummed to wake the troops, drummed to raise the colors, drummed to call for meals, drummed through the drills, drummed to pass the time, and drummed to send everyone to bed. If there was a moment he wasn't eating or sleeping, he was most likely drumming.

It passed the time well, bringing him to dinner where he enjoyed some local beef and cornbread. Dinner was always the best meal, if only because there was no drill duty to run to afterward. Instead, the few evening chores would be done quickly, leaving everyone not on the pickets that night to rest a bit. Sometimes that meant reclining by a fire or making some kind of sport. Other times it meant the entire camp was in bed trying desperately to catch up on sleep.

That particular evening, a nice warm fire was the thing. Charley arrived to find Alfred, Lenny, Chuck, and Joe already there, as well as an older soldier named Abel Tyson and John Coon, the youngest soldier not carrying an instrument. John mustered in from West Chester the same time as Charley, and he had known of the family before they both enlisted. No one knew much about Abel, aside from the fact that he was an ornery sort.

"These Skunks'll have us in an early grave," Abel grumbled. "I swear they can't wait to see us all in a heap."

"Come off it, Abel," Chuck replied. "Jus' cause you can't keep your nose clean doesn't mean anyone is out to get you."

"Skunk?" Charley said, confused by the word.

"Refers to the officers," Chuck explained, "not a very nice way of sayin' it, though. Don't listen to Abel anyways. The old man's wallpapered from sundown to Reveille."

"Whatdya know about it anyway, Baker?"

"You boys mind keepin' it down while I tune?" Lenny cut in, banjo in hand.

Abel rolled his eyes, but didn't make a reply. The rest adjusted their seating to allow Charley and his drum into the circle. Joe gave him a wink from across the fire and Charley smiled.

"Alright, what should we do first?" Lenny asked, finishing up the last string.

"How about 'Lincoln and Liberty'?" Alfred suggested.

"Who ya tryin' to impress, Moulder?" Abel hissed. "Lincoln ain't in earshot, anyways. Not like he's gonna come hear you singin' his praises and make you Secretary of War or somethin'."

"You really don't have to be here," Chuck shot back. "If you're not happy with the music you can crawl back to your bottle, wherever you left it."

"I'm all out," Abel muttered.

"I've got some brandy if you want a swig," John offered eagerly. Abel looked interested, but Chuck shook his head.

"Give that man a swig and he'll down your bottle. Let him take the rest of the night off. We'll all be better for it in the morning. You don't have to bend over backwards to get anyone to like you, John. We're all brothers-in-arms here."

"Thanks, Chuck," John replied. Abel muttered something incomprehensible but didn't put up any further fight.

"'Lincoln and Liberty,' then?" Alfred said.

"Sure enough," Lenny answered. "You know it, Charley?"

"Old Irish tune, yeah?" Charley said. "Pretty sure I know it."

"That's the ticket," Lenny said, and launched into the song. Charley and Joe joined in as the other boys started singing along.

> HURRAH for the choice of the nation!
> Our chieftain so brave and so true;
> We'll go for the great Reformation—
> For Lincoln and Liberty too!
>
> We'll go for the son of Kentucky—
> The hero of Hoosierdom through;
> The pride of the Suckers so lucky—
> For Lincoln and Liberty too!

They continued through the verses and ended in a chorus of raucous cheers when they reached the end. As they did, Sgt. Wallings appeared by the fire among them.

"What's all the rumpus?" he asked. "Startin' the next campaign already, are we?"

"Er, our apologies," Chuck stammered. "Were we being too loud, sergeant?"

"What's that?" Wallings said, taken off guard. "Oh my no, it's after drill time, you boys do as you will. You don't need to be afraid of me if we ain't in ranks. Just make sure you keep the volume up so the captain can hear. He loves a good song, but I doubt he'd ever come out and show it to yer faces."

An audible sigh of relief came from those present, though Charley could still feel the hairs on his neck standing up.

"Why don't you have a seat with us, then," Lenny offered. "We're just making a bit of music to dispel the cold and all."

"Well, I suppose I can spare a few minutes. What's next to sing?"

"Your choice, Don Juan," Alfred said with a grin. Sgt. Wallings turned and froze him with a stare.

"It's Sgt. Wallings or there won't be another note played outside a drill."

Alfred's mouth clamped shut and a few of the others stifled laughter. Wallings was serious, but after a few moments his face softened.

"How about 'Annie Lisle' then," Wallings suggested.

"We're tryin' to raise spirits," Abel spat, "not chase the whole damned company into the Potomac."

"Hush now, Abel," Lenny growled. "Sergeant likes the song. 'Annie Lisle,' then we'll sing 'Oh! Susanna.' Better?"

Abel did not respond, but the decision was made nonetheless. They played 'Annie Lisle,' then 'Oh! Susanna,' and many other songs until it grew too cold to play and the musicians had to move in closer to the fire. Charley reached his hands out next to the flame and felt the warmth reveal the aching pain previously hidden by stiffness and cold. He cringed, but did his best to hide how much it hurt.

"Pretty cold, hey?" Alfred said. "Makes you wonder about what those boys at Valley Forge went through and how any of 'em survived."

"Can't say I've ever wanted to wonder that," Lenny replied.

"Have you ever been to the old encampment?" Alfred asked. "It's not so far from our homes if you're willing to make a day of it."

"Never," Lenny said. "I'll pass on that, thank you."

"It's a bit spooky at night," Chuck put in. "I was no older than six when I went, though. I suppose it's no scarier than the cold is now—or was then."

"I'd take a bullet over a frost any day," Lenny said. "Let me die honorably, at least, if I'm going to meet my maker. You know, it'll be nice to have something to show for it."

"I suppose I'd rather just not die," Charley said, "if I can help it."

The rest of the soldiers laughed, but they had to agree.

"Aye, there's a fine plan," said Sgt. Wallings.

"It's the goal for all of us, isn't it?" Charley shot back. "We won't do much good lying in our graves. I'd at least like to live long enough to pick up a gun and really fight, instead of banging this drum."

The once jovial soldiers grew silent. Charley looked at their faces and wondered what had suddenly made them so wistful. He saw Alfred start to stare down at the dirt, as Wallings examined him with a pained look.

"You know," the sergeant said, "a bare few months ago not a person around this fire, nor truly around this continent, would have guessed this war could ever go on that long. Over in a few months, that's what they said. Now it's maybe a year or two. What happens if we lose the next big battle, eh? Is it four more years? Five more years?

"This army we're with now, for the most part not one of you has seen the battlefield—the place we're going to be for who knows how long. I wish I could roll my eyes at young Charley here, thinking the war

Camp Curtin was named for the Governor of Pennsylvania at the time, Andrew Curtin. Enlisted soldiers from across the state congregated there to train for the coming battles after Lincoln's call for more troops. Prior to the disaster at Bull Run, few in the North expected the war to last more than a year. ("Camp Curtin," in *Harper's Weekly*, September, 1861)

might last until he can lift a gun. But what would that be, four years? Five? Can any of us still say it'll be over before then after Bull Run?"

"I don't suppose we can," Alfred said, his voice a mere whisper. In the silence that followed, Abel Tyson got up and rumbled away. John followed soon after, complaining of the waning heat from the dying fire. A few more dropped off shortly after, the night soured by the looming clouds of war.

Finally, when only the sergeant and Charley were left, Wallings looked at him again.

"I don't mean to belabor the point, boy," he said, "but this is serious business. Once the cannonballs start flying and the muskets start ringin' out, there's no time left to be anything but precise. No time to think about anything but the orders coming from your commander and the men to the right and left of you. Other than that, keep your back straight, play that drum clear, and stay alive. Nothing else matters."

Charley nodded, not sure what he could say in response, but Wallings didn't seem too interested in a conversation. The sergeant always seemed like the most confident man on the field. While Alfred, Charles, Joe, and Lenny felt something like older brothers, Sgt. Wallings seemed more like a father. But in the fire's dim light, his true age showed through. His faraway stare was not that of a seasoned soldier, but of a twenty-year-old man uncertain of what tomorrow would bring.

Charley felt for a moment like he should offer some kind of comforting word, but the feeling passed. He knew better than to press the sergeant further. He said his piece and that was that.

"Run along now, kid," Wallings said, his eyes straining toward the darkness. "I'll take care of the fire."

CHAPTER 7

Marching Orders

March 8, 1862

The morning started in much the same way as the rest, with Charley and Joe waking the troops, playing for the colors, and calling all to breakfast. A courier for Colonel Irwin arrived around mid-morning, but this was not terribly uncommon. However, Charley would come to learn that this was likely the most significant message Captain Sweney had yet received and everything was about to change.

At about eleven in the morning, Capt. Sweney appeared and told Charley to play the order to fall in. Charley did as he was bidden without hesitation, and the rest of the company fell in quickly. There was a deeper look of concern than usual on Capt. Sweney's face, which led to considerable whispering amongst the troops as they assembled, but a sharp word from Wallings caused them all to fall quiet.

Once everyone stood at attention before him, Capt. Sweney stepped forward.

"Men," he said, "I have been very impressed with your progress this winter. I have conveyed to Col. Irwin how proud I am of your hard work and he has passed the message up the chain of command that Company F and, indeed, the entire 49th Pennsylvania Volunteer Regiment is ready for battle. Our commanders, it seems, have agreed. Boys, drill time is over. In a few minutes, we'll be striking camp, forming up with the rest of the regiment, and marching toward Washington, D.C. Once there, we will receive further orders. Until then, you will march, camp, eat, and march some more. Is that understood?"

"Yes, sir!"

"Good. Now there is one more order of business before we strike camp. As I said, Col. Irwin is very pleased with your hard work and as such has decided to honor the man who, by my own suggestion, is chiefly responsible for your successful training. Sgt. Wallings, would you step forward."

A moment of surprise flashed across the sergeant's face, but he stepped forward quickly, his chin raised to the sky.

"Don Juan Wallings, in recognition of your great success, hard work, and dedication to the war effort, you are hereby promoted to the rank of Second Lieutenant. Do you accept this high and well-deserved honor?"

"Of course, Captain," Lt. Wallings replied. Capt. Sweney raised the salute and Wallings followed suit. As the brought their hands down, Capt. Sweney smiled.

"Alright, then, Lieutenant. Give the order."

Wallings turned quickly to face Charley and called out,

"Company, strike tents!"

Charley launched into the cadence without hesitation and the men hurriedly fell out. In a matter of minutes the camp had packed up everything they needed to march. Of course, their winter camp having provided them with covered bunks, there were no tents to strike, but they packed the canvas shelters they would soon live in for the duration of the war and strapped them to their packs. Picking up their weapons last, Company F fell in and waited for their turn to march forward.

As they stood still as statues, Companies A through E marched forward. Charley saw Colonel Irwin atop his horse, watching as his regiment passed by. He felt his back straighten involuntarily at the sight of the colonel and would have laughed at himself were he not intent to keep perfectly still. Since his conversation with now Lt. Wallings by the fire in January, he had made every effort to execute each order, each move, and each cadence with precision. Now that they were finally marching to war, he was not about to allow himself to slip.

At long last, Company E was clear of the path before them and Capt. Sweney gave Charley a nod. He marked time for a moment until Lt. Wallings called out "forward march!" and he launched into the cadence. Joe marched beside him, fife tucked away for the moment. Side by side,

Company F moved forward to the sound of Charley's drum. Capt. Sweney saluted as they passed, and Col. Irwin returned the salute. Charley felt a swelling of pride in his chest. The wait was over. The time had come to enter the war.

★ ★ ★

Two weeks later, the 49th had not quite made it to the war. They had, in fact, only made it to Alexandria, across the Potomac from Washington, D.C. The march had been long and slow, as bad weather bogged down the entire army. For his part, Charley kept an even keel. During the day, they marched. At night, they convened around fires to discuss the day's march. Sometimes they sang, sometimes they simply collapsed once their tents were pitched. In the morning, they would strike camp and move on—day after day, for 14 days.

On March 23, they stood waiting by the river as a steamer made port. Charley could hear the whisperings amongst his fellow soldiers. Capt. Sweney had ordered them at ease while they waited for their next orders. By then, it was common knowledge that they would be boarding the ship and heading south, but Charley did not know where.

"I heard a rumor we're going to try to take back Fort Sumter," Joe offered, but Chuck dismissed this idea.

"Doubtful," he said. "The enemy is in Virginia, so we'll likely meet them there. If we can get to Richmond, we'll strike a pretty harsh blow. Hard to say what General Johnston could do to respond to that. I'll wager we head down toward the Virginia Peninsula and move toward Yorktown."

"The Peninsula," Alfred remarked, "I think I heard something about that. Yorktown would be interesting. Start the end of their rebellion where the real one ended. We can save America twice in the same place."

"Interesting thought," Lenny put in, "but I think we all know it's not just going to end there. No, we'll be fightin' this one for some time."

"Well, if we get Yorktown we're clear to Richmond, don't you think?" Chuck said. "I'm not saying it'll be easy, but the Rebel capital would be quite a prize. Don't you think it would put a pretty big dampener on their morale?"

"Well sure," Lenny replied, "and I'm as optimistic as the next about us winning this war, but I keep thinking about how confident we were before it started. I keep thinking, we were sure these Southern boys would fold faster than a tent, but here we are. Not only are they not licked, they've been winning so far. I just don't think one city is gonna be enough."

"Maybe not," Charley offered, "but it's better than no cities, right?"

"You're right in that," Lenny replied.

"Don't think too far past the next battle," Chuck advised. "If I learned anything from farming, it's that you've gotta focus on each harvest before you plan for the next. Every year changes the soil in one way or another, but if you aren't growing somethin' today, you'll starve before you figure out next year."

A few of the boys nodded, but Charley noticed Alfred chuckling. After a moment, he was rolling into a full-on laugh. The others looked quizzically at him until he finally composed himself.

"What's so funny about that?" Chuck asked.

"I… it's not funny," Alfred confessed, "I was just thinkin' about how farming must be as far a thing from fightin' as there is. But as I thought about it, I realized that's not true in the least. On a farm, you give a bunch of crops life, cultivate them, and then when the time comes you cut 'em all down. Well, we just spent the last six months being cultivated and we'll spend the next six being cut down."

Nearly every jaw in earshot dropped as Alfred finished speaking. Chuck shook his head, eyes wide.

"You're right, Al. That's *not* funny," he said.

"I know," Alfred replied, "I just…"

As he brushed a tear from the edge of his eye, his face fell into stoic ease.

"I got to thinkin' about it and I didn't know how to respond to the thought," he continued. "It just got so absurd, trying to know how to feel about my own thought that I couldn't think of what to do other than laugh."

"It's just nerves," Lenny offered. "Standing here, waiting for something big to happen will get the best of any man. Better it happens now than on the field of battle, don't you think, Chuck?"

"I think we ought to talk about something else," Chuck replied. The others seemed to agree, and they turned the conversation to other things. As they did, though, Charley kept his eyes on Alfred, having been quite taken aback by his outburst. With everyone else's attention now turned away from him, Alfred closed his eyes and took a deep breath. His body shook as he exhaled, though it was barely perceptible to the casual observer. Charley wondered just what was going through his mind at that moment.

When he opened his eyes, though, it was like nothing had ever happened. Alfred broke into a calm smile and looked at Charley. He shrugged and then turned back to the others. Charley did not know what to think of this, but before he could further consider it, Capt. Sweney arrived with their orders.

"Alright men," he shouted. "Form up and get ready to board the steamer. Don't worry about a cadence for this bit, Charley. Just make sure you've got everything you brought. That goes for everyone. We won't be up this way again for quite some time. We've got a nice little landing spot down in Virginia. I hope you like history, because we're headed for Yorktown!"

"Well, asked and answered," Chuck said, as he got his gear together. In a matter of minutes, the company had made its way onto the steamer and staked their claim to a sleeping area. Once they had, they went back out to the deck to watch the rest of the men load on to their respective steamers. As they stood, Lenny appeared among them with his banjo in hand.

"Wish we could get some new tunes in, but there's not much reached us lately," he said. "But I was thinking the boys might like the 'Battle Hymn' as they come aboard. What do you think, Charley?"

"How fast do you want it?" Charley asked.

Lenny plucked out the first few notes of the melody and Charley followed along in the air, getting a feel for the piece. Joe came over and looked as well. Finally, Lenny gave Charley a nod and they started up. As they began to play, those assembled quickly joined in to sing:

Mine eyes have seen the glory of the coming of the Lord;
He is trampling out the vintage where the grapes of wrath are stored;

He hath loosed the fateful lightning of His terrible swift sword:
His truth is marching on.

Glory, glory, hallelujah!
Glory, glory, hallelujah!
Glory, glory, hallelujah!
His truth is marching on.

I have seen Him in the watch-fires of a hundred circling camps,
They have builded Him an altar in the evening dews and damps;
I can read His righteous sentence by the dim and flaring lamps:
His day is marching on.

Glory, glory, hallelujah!
Glory, glory, hallelujah!
Glory, glory, hallelujah!
His truth is marching on.

They continued on through all five verses and then ended the song with a whoop and a shout, followed by a loud chorus of cheers from the soldiers nearby. Someone shouted, "play it again!" and they obliged. All told, they played the new song ten times for their fellow soldiers as they passed by. Each time, those who knew the words sang along at the top of their lungs and there was a great lifting of spirits among those soon to embark.

Out of the corner of his eye, Charley saw Capt. Sweney watching his company. He stood beside Col. Irwin, who was speaking on something that held tightly to the attention of the rest of his captains, but for whatever reason, Sweney was more interested in his own men. There was something distant in his eyes, but also a hard determination in his face. He was there with them as they sang, but also a hundred miles away, gearing up for war.

CHAPTER 8

The Peninsula

Company F of the 49th Pennsylvania Volunteer Regiment disembarked their steamer at Fort Monroe on Tuesday, March 25. The fort was a little over 20 miles from Yorktown, and they began their march immediately. The weather, coupled with the size of the army, slowed progress. There was little discussion about the coming battles, as the men kept their focus on the task at hand.

On March 27, foot-weary and grumbling, they found themselves beside a swamp, which the 43rd New York had had the misfortune to trample into. Several members of that regiment got themselves stuck in mud all the way up to their waist. Charley and his fellow Pennsylvanians found it hard not to laugh at the others. More than anything, they appreciated the opportunity to stop and rest. It was nearing time to make camp and there wasn't a soldier present that wasn't weary of the day.

Col. Irwin, though, saw it as an irritating delay. He argued with the other colonel for several minutes until both men were red in the face.

"Hard to see what could have been done differently," Joe muttered. "We get our marching orders from the top, don't we? How's he going to just decide to change them?"

"One might think he could order a halt before they fell into a swamp, no?" Charley replied, trying to fight back a smile. "I do hope they teach the boys how to swim in New York, because they sure need it now."

"Serves 'em right," Abel muttered. "A bunch of city boys walkin' around with their heads in the clouds."

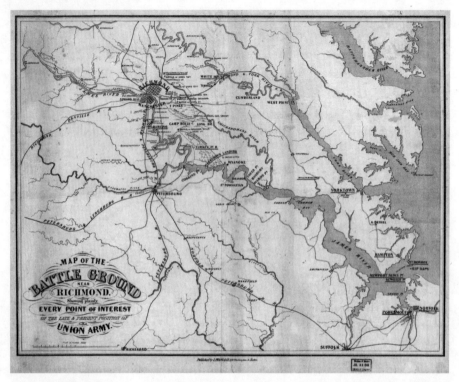

The strategic importance of Richmond cannot be overstated. Beyond being the capital of the Confederacy, it was also a major railroad hub used to move troops and supplies throughout the South. At the outbreak of the war, two different sized railroad tracks were in use. Most tracks heading north from Richmond used 4' 8" gauge tracks, while most heading south used 5' tracks. This meant moving troops and supplies from the deep south to Northern Virginia (where most of the fighting took place) required changing trains in Richmond. By capturing the city, the Union could theoretically isolate the Army of Northern Virginia, a crippling blow to a Confederate cause that was already suffering through the complete Union blockade of their ports. (Map produced by W. H. Forbes & Co., Boston, 1863)

"Come off it, ya old fart," Alfred hissed. "They're on our side… sure look like a bunch of fools right now, though."

"Wet fools," Joe chimed in.

The 43rd was just getting its bearings back when a hush fell over all the assembled troops. Col. Irwin noticed and spun around to find none other than General Hancock riding toward them.

"What the hell are you doing there?" he cried out.

Both Irwin and the New York colonel grew sheepish and scrounged for something to say, but as they stood silent, one of the New York boys called out from the swamp,

"Just hunting my boots, General! Think I spotted some tracks over yonder. Not sure how they made 'em without me in 'em, though!"

A round of laughter rippled through both regiments and Hancock shook his head. He looked down at the colonels.

"Well, what the hell's the matter?" he asked, as the regiment continued to laugh.

"Oh! It's the bad state of the ground, sir," Col. Irwin replied.

"Bad hell!" Hancock growled. "It's the bad luck of the regiment."

Turning his horse, he rode down the line. As he passed Company D, he called back to the colonels,

"Well, will I have to be general, colonel, captain, sergeant and corporal?"

"We don't care a damn," someone called out from the crowd, "only so you let us camp!"

The whole of both regiments gave three cheers in support of the suggestion, and General Hancock turned his horse about. He looked over the soldiers before him and then up into the failing light above. After a few moments, he looked to the two colonels still standing nearby.

"Make camp, boys. We'll march extra hard tomorrow. I suppose you boys in the 43rd should look for a dryer spot."

General Hancock rode off without another word as Col. Irwin gave the order to make camp. The boys were glad to have a rest, but the next day brought more of the same. Slow marches, wide swamps, and more tired feet.

By March 31, they reached Newport News. They were still a way out of Yorktown but the path had eased some. They were finished with swamps, it seemed, and onto much less hostile terrain. Of course, terrain was not the hostility they needed to worry about.

Camped outside Newport News, Company F sat around a dozen fires resting their feet and enjoying a few songs from Lenny, Charley, and Joe. When their voices grew tired, they sat in quiet conversation as the stars appeared above their heads.

"We're drawing near now," Chuck said, with a faraway gaze.

"We've been drawing near for weeks," Lenny shot back. "Are we slowing down or is Yorktown growing farther away?"

"Slow going," Alfred said, "but we'll be there soon enough. Why don't you sing another song?"

"Don't feel much like it," Lenny replied.

"What about you, Charley," Alfred asked. "Want to drum something soft?"

Charley did not reply. He was turning his left ear to the sky, trying to capture the strange whistling sound he could swear was approaching.

"Do you hear…"

In a moment, there was no question of what was approaching. Not far from their encampment, a shell exploded. The men were on their feet in an instant as another shell came tumbling through the sky.

"Should we form ranks?" Charley shouted. "What should we do?"

"Take cover!" Chuck cried out. "Wait for orders if there'll be any!"

"We should get the hell out of here!" Abel yelled, looking frantically from side to side.

"Enough of that," said Lt. Wallings, appearing amongst them. "It's one blasted ship, can't you see that? It'll be run off in a matter of minutes. Sit tight and move if you see somethin' coming."

"How can we see anything in the dark?" Alfred asked.

"Well, you're right," Wallings replied with a sarcastic tone. "I guess you won't be able to dodge a thing, so you might as well just sit tight. How about that?"

Alfred simply ducked down in reply, shaking his head as he muttered something incomprehensible. Charley moved closer to Wallings, keeping his head down as well.

"Is this what a battle feels like?" he asked, immediately regretting the question. Wallings looked down at him with a dry laugh.

"This is a Sunday in the park compared to a real battle, Charley. Get some sleep. We're not about to slow down if they're sending little ships after us."

★ ★ ★

As it turned out, that was the last of the Rebel ships sent to shell their troops. The rest of the march continued largely without incident until April 8 when General Hancock ordered the general halt five miles outside of the city. Charley rose to his tiptoes to try to see the city, but it was still quite far off in the distance. When he could not make out much of anything, he frowned and dropped back down. Chuck was standing behind him and leaned over.

"Nothing much to see anyway," he said, "though that's kind of the point."

"What do you mean?" Charley asked.

"If we can see the Rebels, they can see us. It wouldn't make a whole lot of sense to make camp right in plain view, even if we are laying siege to the city. If even a handful of those boys has a Whitworth rifle, we'll be hearin' hornets buzzing by our ears all day—if we're lucky..."

"Oh... do you think we'll try to take the city soon?"

"Likely not right away," Chuck replied. "More likely the bulk of us'll spend the next few days on picket duty. I doubt you'll be assigned. It ain't the safest job."

Chuck was entirely right, Charley soon found out, as several men from Company F were assigned to the first picket duty the next day. Chuck, Lenny, John, Abel, and Alfred all left early that morning to form a scattered line on the outskirts of the camp, leaving Joe and Charley behind. There was not much for the two of them to do, so they spent much of the day playing quietly together. As the sun sank toward the horizon, though, the others came home looking weary and covered in dirt.

"I don't think I shall ever experience anything so simultaneously dull, dangerous, and exhausting in my life as picket duty," Abel grumbled, as he collapsed onto the ground in a heap.

"For once, I'm inclined to agree with Mr. Tyson," Lenny said. "I swear I dodged ten, maybe eleven shots from those snipers across the way. Damned if I couldn't hear them laughing at me rollin' about."

"You didn't dodge a thing," Chuck muttered, "they missed. You can't dodge a sniper bullet, Lenny."

"Maybe *you* can't," Lenny replied, "but I'm quite nimble."

"I saw you stumble into two separate ditches since we landed in Virginia," Alfred chuckled. "The Rebel boys probably just felt sorry for you."

This elicited a weak laugh from a few of the others, but mostly there were only exhausted groans. John Coon looked quite worse for wear as he laid himself on the grass beside the fire Chuck was making.

"I've got splinters all over from laying on that stand," he said. "Where on earth did they get that wood? There's more in me than there is left in the field."

"At least you got to hide in a stand," Alfred replied. "My post was under a blasted bush. A *thorn* bush. I'm likely to bleed to death from a thousand little pricks."

"Better that than a bullet," Lenny grumbled. "It's just not sporting, shooting a man from a thousand yards away. Line up in front of me like a man and we'll both give it our best shot, eh? Out there, I just feel like a fool who may as easily die of boredom."

"Maybe they'll let you take your banjo out next time," Alfred said with a grin.

"Oof, them snipers sure won't keep tryin' to miss then," Chuck put in.

"*I* might shoot him myself," Abel muttered.

"Oh can it, Tyson," Lenny shot back. "No one asked you."

Abel huffed but made no retort. The men back from picket duty stayed awake long enough to eat supper, and then most of them headed off to bed. They would go out on picket duty twice more over the next ten days. In the meantime, the most grueling duty assigned to Charley was the nights where he was tasked with standing ready for the long roll.

When encamped so close to the enemy, it was necessary for at least one drummer in the regiment to remain awake overnight should any enemy movement require the boys to form up in ranks. If any report warranted such an action, whichever officer was in command that night would order the drummer to strike the long roll, which was exactly what it sounded like. Charley would have to play loud and long until the entire regiment was up and at the ready. For his first turn at the overnight watch, everything was silent. The same could not be said for April 18.

Charley sat awake as he was required to do, while the others were beginning to snore in their tents. The night was crisp, but not cold, as the Virginia spring was more temperate than his native Pennsylvania. As he sat there trying his best to keep alert, he thought over the year that had passed. A little more than a year ago the war had started and Charley had yet to see action. Little more than a year ago...

"Oh!" Charley said, surprising himself. "I missed my birthday!"

"Well that won't do," came Lenny's voice from behind. Charley turned around in time to see the man approach and take a seat beside him.

"I couldn't sleep," Lenny explained. "I know it's another four days before we're back out on picket, but I'm dreading it all the same. So, you're thirteen now, is it?"

"That's right," Charley replied. "I can't believe I forgot about my own birthday. Back home I would be thinking about it for weeks ahead of time."

"Well, long days of the same old thing can do that. Truth be told, I wasn't quite sure what day it was, myself. Friday, I think."

"Friday is right," Charley confirmed. "It's just amazing what you do and don't think of when you're out here. I spent more time considering the creases of my uniform for inspection this morning than I have thinking about home all week. I miss it, but it feels so far away that I can't even imagine being back there."

"Well, that'll come back," Lenny said, "and when it does, it'll hit ya hard. Don't worry, though, we'll all be here for you when it does."

"Thanks, I..."

Charley's thought was cut short by the sound of musket-fire in the distance. He jumped to his feet, his drum already strapped over his shoulder. Lenny rose more slowly and peered out into the darkness. After a moment, they heard another sound from the left and turned to see Capt. Sweney approaching quickly.

"Long roll, Charley," he shouted. "Wake 'em up!"

Charley was into the roll before Sweney even finished the order. Men rushed out of their tents in full uniform, hurrying to fall into ranks. Within minutes, the entire regiment was ready and awaiting orders. Colonel Irwin appeared already on horseback looking flush with excitement. As the musket-fire continued, he called out the order to advance and the regiment took to the road.

Some grumbling was heard as they began to move, largely from Abel, but the men marched as they were told, headed toward General Hancock's headquarters and on toward the sounds of battle. They paused when they reached the headquarters and saw the general himself emerging

"General," Col. Irwin called out, "I have run the 49th out left in front, so that you will have the regiment handy."

As he spoke, the general's face grew red.

"Damn you, colonel!" he shouted back. "Run the 49th back right in front and stay there until you receive orders to come! What is the point of being a general if you can't even get a colonel to follow orders!"

"I… yes sir," Irwin replied, sheepishly. "Sorry, sir. I'll return the men as you have ordered. I only meant to… well… as you ordered, sir, we'll march on back."

General Hancock grumbled something as Colonel Irwin gave the order to turnabout. The men had to stifle their laughter at the sight of the now flustered Irwin hurrying back toward camp. The laughter quickly soured, however, when the skies opened up and rain began to pour down on them. Their moods fell even further as camp came into view, for at the very same time a bugle call from General Smith's headquarters drew them over to his position in relief. In relief of what, none could say, as they spent the next hour standing still in the dark and rain, waiting for action that never came.

At that point, the musket-fire had stopped and the night was quiet once again. After a long march that led to nothing, the men were dismissed back to their camp. The entire company, save Charley and Lenny, were asleep in their dampened clothes within minutes. Charley and Lenny returned to their positions, unallowed and unable to sleep, respectively. Instead, they talked quietly to one another to pass the time.

"Unpleasant as the night is, I should like to have at least come close to whatever battle awoke the regiment," Lenny said. "I must admit that this camp has driven me a fair bit stir-crazy. If we don't attack or move camp soon, I may lose my already meager mind."

"I think the entire camp agrees with you," Charley replied. "Do you remember what we were talking about before the long roll was ordered?"

"Haven't a clue," Lenny confessed. "My mind doesn't hold on to much for very long these days. All I've got up there is marching maneuvers and a couple dozen songs. I suppose that's all a simple soldier needs room for, eh?"

"I suppose so," Charley replied. "We don't play as much as we used to."

"I know," Lenny said. "But we will. When the tension breaks and the battles really start, we'll need it. Everyone will need a little music to settle the mind."

"I'll be glad to be a part of it."

"There are few greater honors," Lenny said, smiling from ear to ear.

CHAPTER 9

April 22, 1862

The morning of April 22 brought another picket duty for forty men from Company F—Lenny, Chuck, Alfred, John, and Abel among them. Charley and Joe stayed at camp, as usual, and passed the time either practicing or talking idly. By mid-afternoon, Charley was wiping down his drum, though it had barely a speck of dirt on it.

"I think I might be at the end of my rope," Joe said. "I spend every hour of the day just trying to pass the time, and at night I can't hardly fall asleep expecting to hear that long roll start up any minute. Every time I hear a musket fire I'm certain this is it, but it ain't."

"We must be planning to move in soon," Charley replied. "It's been over two weeks. We can't just wait here forever. Does General Smith expect the Rebs just to give up the city?"

"Couldn't tell ya," Joe answered. "All I know is I'm fairly certain Lenny's gonna lose his mind if has to go out on picket one more time. I don't blame them, either, the way they talk about it. Hours at a time just watching, waiting to see if someone is gonna come across the field at you. Then if they do, you had better hoof it quick or you'll be dead where you lay. I heard a sniper got two guys from the New York 43rd the other day."

"I heard that wasn't true," Charley shot back, "but who knows, I guess. It's a believable enough rumor."

"It's bound to happen eventually, if not already. I just hope it doesn't happen to one of our Pennsylvania boys. Company F can't spare a soldier, far as I'm concerned."

"Yeah," Charley said, seeing a line of men approaching from across the field. "Here they come now."

The picketmen from Company F came trudging forward, their faces looking heavier than usual. Charley thought it must have been a rough day, but there was something deeper. He watched them approach and rose to his feet when they were near. Alfred and Chuck barely seemed to notice him as they passed by, and that's when he realized what was so odd.

"Where's Lenny?"

Alfred stopped and looked back at him, his face falling even lower. He opened his mouth to speak, but instead just shook his head.

"Did he get injured?" Charley asked. "Did they take him to the hospital tent or what? What's going on?"

"The bugger's dead," Abel grumbled. Chuck whirled around at the words and moved as if to strike Abel, but Alfred caught his arm.

"There's been enough hurt today," he said. "Let the old goat go on and be miserable by himself."

"I'd like to put him in the ground instead of…" Chuck hissed, but his voice drifted off as he spoke.

"I don't understand," Charley said, "was there a fight we didn't hear about? Did Johnny Reb come firing at you? We didn't hear any shots."

"It wasn't Johnny Reb," Alfred sighed. "He's… he did it himself, I suppose. Not on purpose mind you but… damn it, Lenny."

"What? What happened? You have to tell me!" Charley pleaded. Alfred just shook his head and turned away. Chuck gave him a pained look, but did not speak, and John let out a weak whimper.

"It's gonna be all of us sooner or later," John said. "We'll all be dead and buried soon, just like Lenny. Whether we stay here or march to battle, we're doomed to the ground."

"Hush up, John," was all Chuck could say, and he made his way back to the tent. The rest of the company continued away without so much as a word to Charley or Joe. The two musicians stood dumbfounded, looking to one another for an answer neither had.

"I don't understand," Joe whispered. "What happened?"

Charley shook his head, but then he had an idea.

"I don't know," he said, "but I bet Capt. Sweney does."

Without further discussion, Charley hurried off in search of the captain. He found him standing by his tent, reading some orders he must have recently received. Charley waited patiently at attention while he finished reading and handed the paper off to Lt. Wombacker and bid him take care of things. Then, he nodded to Charley.

"At ease, Mr. King. What can I do for you?"

"What happened to Lenny?" Charley blurted out. Capt. Sweney looked perplexed at the outburst.

"What happened to whom?"

"Lenny," Charley repeated. "Um, Private Leonard Appleman. He was on picket duty and he didn't come back this evening. The others said… they said they buried him."

"Oh," Capt. Sweney muttered, "Pvt. Appleman, yes. I'm afraid he was killed on picket duty around mid-morning. It's a dangerous duty, but necessary for the protection of the larger army. Were you friends with the private?"

"Yes!" Charley nearly shouted, "he was one of my *best* friends. We would play music together. He's got a banjo, see, and he asked me to play with him. And we played the 'Battle Hymn of the Republic'—you know, on the boat? Did you see that?"

"I did," Captain Sweney replied. "I'm sorry to have lost him. I wasn't aware that his friends called him Lenny. Do you happen to know if his family called him that as well? It is my solemn duty as his commanding officer to write home informing them of his death. I would think that sort of familiarity would soften the blow."

"I don't… maybe? Alfred knew him before the war," Charley explained, "he might know better than I. But you seem so calm. Why are you not more upset?"

"That I lost a man at war?" Sweney said. "I daresay I will lose many. You read me wrongly, though, Charley. I am quite upset at the loss of Pvt. Appleman, but how is a captain to respond to such a thing? I can show nothing but strength and resolve, Charley, regardless of what I feel, or risk losing the esteem in which I am held. You understand?"

"I… suppose. But he wasn't even in battle, sir. He was on picket duty."

"Charley, son," Capt. Sweney said, "there is something you must realize. Since the day we landed in Virginia, we have been in battle. There are fewer bullets and fewer deaths on days like this, but that does not mean there are none. Picket duty is dangerous. That's part of the reason you were not assigned to it. Those on picket are the first to face the enemy should they approach, they are under watch from snipers, and they may be attacked at any minute."

"So, Lenny was killed by a sniper?" Charley asked.

"Well," Capt. Sweney sighed, "no, he was not. Unfortunately, accidents also happen while out on picket duty. It is my understanding that, while attempting to repair a lookout blind, Pvt. Appleman lost his footing. He fell fifteen feet onto his head and, from what I was told, broke his neck on impact. Your friend was tragically dead before anyone could reach him. I'm sorry."

Captain Sweney donned a sympathetic look, and Charley struggled to find words. He shook his head, dumbfounded that Lenny had died in such a manner.

"All he wanted was for the battle to happen so he would be through waiting," he said. "Instead, he died waiting."

"I've decided I shall not tell his family the specific manner in which he died," Capt. Sweney said. "I will say only that he was killed carrying out my orders and that we are all safe for his actions. Nothing more seems necessary to burden them with."

Charley could not bring himself to think of Lenny's family. Just knowing his friend was gone hurt plenty.

"I didn't know men could die like that in war. I thought it was something that happened to old men and drunkards."

"There are many things in this world that can kill a soldier," Capt. Sweney replied. "Bullets and cannons, yes, but also accidents and sickness. Some men will die of cold when winter returns. Some may even collapse from exhaustion in the heat of summer. There is only so much anyone can do to stop it."

"I see," Charley said, casting his eyes toward the ground. "You promised my father you would keep me safe. Is that really a promise you can keep?"

Capt. Sweney turned away, sucking his teeth as he looked off into the distance.

"You best return to your tent, Charley," he said. "It'll be nighttime soon."

Without another word, Capt. Sweney walked off, leaving Charley no choice but to do as he suggested. He trudged back across the camp to where Joe sat alone, fiddling with his fife. As he approached, Charley began to recognize the song Joe was playing. He had heard it many a time before at church with his parents, filling the rafters as the faithful sang together. But today, it felt thin, played weakly into the endless sky above.

Charley tried for a moment tried to sing along, but all he could manage was to quietly whisper,

"Nearer, my God to thee..." before he fell silent again, simply listening to the quiet tune. As the song came to an end, Charley wept. And he did not care who saw.

CHAPTER 10

Williamsburg

May 5, 1862

"Did you hear what he said?" Charley shouted to Joe, as both craned their necks to look at the hot air balloon hovering over their heads.

"Sounded like the pebbles left?" Joe replied, "but the darned cannon fire is making it hard to hear anything."

"He said the Rebels left!" Captain Sweney shouted. "Sound the long roll, Charley. Guns and equipment only boys. This is it!"

Charley stood stunned, unable to think, but his hands acted without pause. He beat out the long roll and the men scattered to grab their weapons. Within two minutes, they all fell in and Capt. Sweney gave the order to march. They moved off double-quick down the road toward the Rebel positions. Charley looked across the line at his company, studying their faces as battle approached.

Chuck was stone-faced and determined, clutching his musket to his chest as he ran, eyes locked ahead. Alfred was beside him, similarly determined but also betraying a hint of fear. They all felt it, Charley knew, but some hid the feeling better than others. For his part, he saw no need to hide it at all. He was afraid, but he would not waver. He was beside his friends, helping to lead troops to battle just as he had dreamed. This was the moment he had envisioned so many times before.

They crossed over a small dam as they went along, and Charley heard someone yell,

"This is it, boys. Rebeldom!"

For the first time, Charley and Company F were headed into Rebel-held territory. They were headed into battle.

Just a few moments after they crossed, however, shouting echoed from the front of the line. Capt. Sweney wheeled around and shouted, "Halt, boys! Halt!"

The regiment came lurching to a stop and everyone looked quizzically at one another. Chuck, the tallest of the bunch, got on his tiptoes and looked out over the fields.

"Are they out there?" Alfred asked. "Are we making lines? What's going on, Chuck?"

"Nothing," Chuck replied. "The cowards turned tail. But why aren't we in pursuit?"

The question was answered moments later when Colonel Irwin appeared and the captains of the 49th assembled around him.

"The damned Rebels buried a load of shells in the middle of the road," he explained. "I reckon they hoped we were foolish enough to march over them and thin out our own numbers. They failed there, but they've sure slowed us. General Hancock is ordering up some of the prisoners to dig the blasted things up so we can continue down the road, but we'll be stuck here for some time. Put your boys at ease, but stay in ranks. No one breaks the column. The minute we can move again, we'll be off double-quick."

The captains nodded and turned back to relay the order to their companies. Charley unslung his drum and placed it on the ground in front of him.

"So much for the battle," he said.

"Stay alert," Captain Sweney replied. "We'll be on to the Rebels eventually, even if we have to march right up to Fort Magruder, knock on the door, and ask them nicely to come out and fight. We'll be on the move again soon enough."

Soon enough turned out to be midday. With the shells removed from the road, the army continued on, covering four miles by 3 pm. Charley examined the fortifications the Rebels had built and then abandoned along the side of the road as they marched. They were impressive constructions, made of rail metal and brush. There were several camps along the route as well, with tents and commissaries left behind. It appeared, however, that most things of value had been destroyed when the Rebels fled.

By 8 pm, the only sign of the Rebels had been a number of deserters who had the misfortune to come upon their position after abandoning their own. Already broken of their will, they surrendered on sight and were taken to the back of the line as the long column of the corps continued on. With night falling, though, they would have to stop soon and find a place to bed down.

They finally stopped in a field where they could see the lights of Williamsburg flickering in the far distance. Dark as it was, Charley could not make out much more than those few lights. There were fires ahead, not far off, but it was too difficult to tell what they were seeing. Company D advanced to the skirmish line where they would likely spend the entire night to protect against a surprise attack. As the rest of the regiment hunkered down, they could hear the trudging of more troops to their right.

"Who is that?" Charley whispered. "Who's coming?"

"If it were Rebels, we would know by now," Chuck said. "That's the whole point of the skirmish line."

"It ought to be the 6th Maine," Capt. Sweney informed them from nearby. "Hancock sent them up to hold the right flank. You boys keep it quiet through the night, you understand? I don't expect you to sleep, but don't go disturbing the entire regiment gabbing on."

"Yes, Captain," both replied.

The night was ghastly dark, and Charley could barely make out his own hand in front of his face. All he could see were fires in the distance, though it was hard to tell exactly where they were. Sometime in the middle of the night, however, he noticed flickering light beginning to spread through an area not far from where the skirmishers had been dispatched.

"The woods are on fire," he whispered.

"Unless you're on fire yourself, keep quiet," Capt. Sweney replied.

Charley fell silent once more and spent the rest of the evening without uttering so much as an audible sigh. His eyes grew quite heavy, but sleep never found him and, as the first rays of dawn crept over the horizon, he felt great anticipation growing in his heart. It coupled with fear and poise and, as he lay in the dewy grass, he knew he was ready.

He also soon knew what many of the lights ahead of them were, as the dawn revealed the earthen walls of Fort Magruder not three hundred yards in front of them. Rain was falling as the regiment formed up, and the men were thoroughly soaked through, but they were ready to march nonetheless. In the distance, they could see another Union Division begin marching toward the left of the fort. As they neared Williamsburg, there was an eruption of cannon and musket fire. The battle had begun.

A moment later, Colonel Irwin gave the order to move, and the brigade headed for the extreme right of the fort. Charley drummed out orders with Joe playing by his side, as the regiment double-timed it toward their new position. Company D moved out ahead as skirmishers once more and took a nearby hill. Charley could see General Hancock riding up to the base of the hill as the men from Company D looked out over the battlefield.

"Well?" Hancock called out. "What do you see? Who has the fort?"

"They don't know who's occupying the fort?" Abel scoffed. "What are we..."

"Belay the chatter!" Sweney yelled, and Abel fell silent. As the regiment stood by, they heard the general call out again.

"Well? Rebel or Federal?"

One of the men from Company D hurried down the hill and came to a sliding stop in the grass not ten feet away and shouted,

"General, they are damned Rebels!"

A roar of laughter rolled over the regiment followed by a chorus of cheers welcoming the battle now moments away. General Hancock ordered the battery up and the infantrymen moved aside to allow the cannons to advance. As they took their positions, Captain Sweney leaned in close to Charley.

"You might want to cover your ears," he said. Charley turned to the captain to see a broad smile on his face.

"Are you going to cover your ears, sir?" Charley asked.

Captain Sweney laughed.

"How would that look?"

"Then I won't either," Charley said. "How much louder could it be at this distance than a drum right here at my waist?"

Charley's question was answered seconds later as the roar of cannon fire split the air, causing him to drop his sticks and throw his hands up over his ears. The shells soared through the air, arcing high above the earthen redoubts before falling into the fort and exploding on contact. Charley drew his hands back down and looked up at the captain. He could feel his face grow red.

"You'll get used to it," Sweney said. "Or you'll go deaf and it won't bother you at all."

Charley chuckled and braced himself for the next launch. As their shells exploded inside the fort, the Rebels released a volley back toward them. The entire regiment braced themselves for the incoming ordinance, with some taking a few steps back despite the order to hold position. For his part, Charley stood tall, ready for what was about to come. He felt himself tense up, but, as the shells began to fall, he immediately relaxed. Every single Rebel shell fell at least 200 yards short of the line.

Charley heard his fellow soldiers laugh at the enemy's miscalculation— though likely more out of relief than actual good humor. To the right and up the hill, the skirmishers began to open fire on the Rebels, but Charley could not make out what line they were firing upon. Beyond the cannon fire and occasional volleys from the skirmishers, the right side of the battle was largely quiet.

On the far side of the fort, however, the situation was entirely different. The other division, which Charley learned was being led by General Hooker, was taking heavy fire. They could hear the battle from their position as it raged on. Finally, Hooker made a hard push to take the fort from the left side, and Charley and the others watched on with bated breath as they moved forward.

General Hancock's battery kept up its barrage as the battle continued on the far side of the fort. Hooker, for his part, led his men bravely, but it soon became clear that they would be unable to take the day. Finally, towards mid-afternoon, his troops withdrew and fell back to their previous spot. Charley watched as the Rebel forces broke from their shelter and pursued the Union troops. At the same time, a messenger arrived from

General Sumner with an order to fall back. General Hancock looked at the messenger incredulously.

"Fall back? Like hell I'll fall back, these men are ready to fight," he shouted. "Longstreet isn't falling back. He's advancing. To hell with those orders!"

The messenger hurried off in a huff and General Hancock started barking orders. He pulled Company D back, and they slowly made their way to the line. As they did so, a detachment of Rebel cavalry came charging out of a nearby tree line. The men wheeled about and held their ranks as the captains shouted their orders. The cavalry sprang forward and a long line of infantrymen followed after them. When they drew near, however, the cavalry turned hard and sprinted away from the line.

"What the devil was that about?" Chuck muttered. "Why fake a charge?"

"Only the cavalry part was fake," Alfred shouted. The infantrymen kept coming as General Hancock ordered the battery to quickly turnabout. They found their new targets just as the Rebels began to charge forward, hollering at the tops of their lungs.

Once they were in clear range, the battery opened fire with grapeshot and canister, tearing huge holes in the Rebel line. As they began to slow, the Union boys raised their weapons in preparation. Charley could do nothing but watch, the sound of battle filling his ears. There it was, right in front of him, the advancing army and his comrades at arms prepared to meet them. He could already hear the cloud of bullets zipping through the air as the Rebel boys came surging forward. They were nearly...

"Charley!" Captain Sweney called out over the din. "The retreat, boy. Sound the retreat."

"W-what?" Charley replied, quickly becoming flustered. "Retreat?"

"Hancock's called the retreat in alternative, boy. On with it!"

Shaken from his confusion, Charley beat out the cadence. The soldiers around him were shocked for a moment, but quickly fell in line and followed orders. The entire regiment fell back quickly as the Rebels pursued. He could hear the enemy cheering as though the day had been won, but every soldier in blue knew the gambit. They rushed back as quickly as they could with cannon and musket shot buzzing around them.

When they had retreated near a hundred yards, the regiment halted abruptly and turned to face the charging Rebels. Taken aback by the sudden change of tactic, the Rebels slowed a moment, becoming disorganized in their confusion. In those few moments, the entire regiment took up position and lowered their muskets toward the advancing Southerners. Barely a few seconds passed before the order was given, and the long line of Federal men opened fire.

In a flash, the air was alive with the smell of gunpowder and the heat of flame. From his vantage point at the rear of the line, Charley watched nearly three dozen Rebel soldiers drop in an instant. Another volley followed quickly before the Rebels could return fire. Not far from where he stood, Charley saw General Hancock looking over the battle, shouting out orders as the rest of the troops found their positions. As he stood there, a lieutenant from another company hurried up to him and shouted,

"General, you are exposing yourself!"

From atop his horse, Hancock looked down at the man, freezing him with a cold stare.

"Mitchell," he said, "if you are afraid, go to the rear. For my part, I am going to stay here and form this line of battle before I go back."

Mitchell made no further comment and instead hurried back to his own company. The battle continued as smoke from the firearms began to obscure the field. Charley could barely make out the front of their own line, let alone the enemy. Still, the sound of musket balls and shot soaring through the air told him that Johnny Reb had not yet withdrawn. The 49th did not flinch either.

Then, as suddenly as it had started, the firing ceased and the smoke cleared from the battlefield. Many of the Rebel boys ahead of the line had dropped down and thrown their weapons away. Their main force, however, moved off double-quick to the left toward the dam crossing. Without hesitation, General Hancock gave the order to fire upon the enemy troops and it was soon clear to the Rebels they had no chance to hold the crossing. The rest of their regiment fled the field.

Once the firing had stopped, Company D from the 49th broke ranks and headed into the field. Led by Captain Campbell, they were tasked with pushing the fleeing Rebels back further. When the field was cleared, they began gathering discarded arms and collecting the Rebels who had surrendered. Charley watched as they formed those who could walk into a line and marched them away from the field. As they passed, Lt. Wallings leaned over to one of the enemy soldiers.

"Where ya from, soldier," he asked.

"North Carolina, sir. 5th Regiment," the soldier replied.

"I knew a girl from North Carolina once," Wallings said. "Prettiest girl I ever did see."

"I'd rather face down the wartiest hag in the South than your blasted muskets again," the soldier confessed.

"Right-o, soldier. That'd be fine with me. Carry on, then."

The prisoners continued away as the rest of Company D began to gather the Rebel wounded. Charley watched them as they worked, noticing quite a few checking the pockets of the fallen soldiers as they prepared to move them. He frowned as he witnessed some pulling buttons and buckles from those lying on the field and stowing them away in their own munitions bags.

"They're stealing from the wounded," Charley said. "Are they allowed to do that?"

"They'd be relieved of their goods at the stockade anyway," Chuck explained. "I don't suppose it does that much harm to take a few things now. And besides, most of these boys will have passed by the dawn. They've no need for their trinkets."

Charley was disturbed by Chuck's callous reply, but he could think of no words to respond to it. From his side, he saw that Alfred, too, was surprised at what Chuck said.

"I would have hoped we could hold on to our honor past at least a single battle," Alfred said.

"Honor is won at the end of a musket," Chuck shot back, "and besides, what can be honorable about the men who lie before us? Rebels. Slavers. Traitors."

"And we are none of the three," Alfred said. "And so it is with honor that we should carry ourselves."

Chuck grumbled but made no further argument. He instead seemed content to watch the wounded Rebels be carried away. The battle was a victory, if only for General Hancock. Charley heard the report from their part of the day as it was told to Col. Irwin. Nearly 90 Rebels killed, 90 to 100 wounded, and all told about 165 taken prisoner. The 49th lost fewer than 40 men overall.

Company F did not lose one.

The day came to an end much as it had started. A heavy drizzle soaked the entire landscape and every man who had fought that day. Wet and cold as he was, Charley could not help but smile. He had survived his first battle.

And won.

CHAPTER II

The Lull

May 7, 1862

Charley slept surprisingly well the night after the battle, though that was likely helped by his lack of sleep the night before. The dawn brought with it relative silence, as the camp was slow to stir for the morning call. It was the first true action for the vast majority of the corps and the toll it took on the 49th was clear as day. Even Chuck looked wary of what might come along with the sunlight.

The boys of Company F spent most of the morning sitting by their campfires awaiting orders. A few of the other companies were sent down to help with clearing the fields, while a good number went out on picket duty. More than usual were set out, as the Rebel Army was still somewhere in the area, but things remained quiet throughout the day.

Early in the afternoon, orders came down through Colonel Irwin that Company F, along with Company D, were to report to the hospital currently reserved for captured Rebels to help out. There were some rumblings amongst the men over the idea of helping the injured Rebels, but Col. Irwin's stern stare silenced them. Without further protest, they made their way to the hospital.

Before they reached it, they were confronted with the sight of a few hundred bloodied and broken Southern soldiers. Charley gasped when he saw the lines of wounded men that awaited them. Many were left by themselves as there were not nearly enough medics to tend to them all. One man reached out to him as he passed, and Charley looked down to see blood seeping from his eye. He was frozen in place for a moment before Alfred caught his arm and pulled him away.

"Best not to look until you have to," he said.

"Belay that," Chuck muttered. "Take it in, Charley. This is what we're here for. You're going to see a lot more of it as the days go past."

"What's gotten into you, Chuck?" Alfred shot back. "Ever since Lenny died you've been sour as a green apple. We all lost a friend."

"And we all move on," Chuck cut in. "Pardon me if I've decided to be a little more focused on what's in front of me."

A moment of silence passed, before the hard look began to fade from Chuck's face. He shook his head and looked down at the bodies all around them.

"Maybe it just made this all real before I was ready," Chuck admitted. "Seeing him lying there dead... none of these Rebel boys means a lick of what Lenny meant to me. Maybe I'm happy to be buryin' 'em."

No one knew what to say, so they said nothing. Despite Alfred's suggestion, Charley looked down at a wounded Rebel who lay nearby. The soldier was unconscious, with a long red stain running down from his head, across his cheek, and onto his neck. Charley wondered if he would ever wake up again or if he was simply waiting to die... and how long would it take?

Shaking his head, Charley pushed the thought away just as the commander of the medic corps approached them. Lt. Wallings stepped forward and saluted.

"Reporting for duty, sir," he said. "Lt. Don Juan Wallings, with Companies F and D of the 49th Pennsylvania Regiment. At your service, sir."

"I appreciate it, Lieutenant," the medic replied. "I wish I had a more pleasant duty for you but these boys have got to be moved from the field. If you find any of them have expired during their wait, leave 'em be for now. We'll have to bury the lot of them at some point, but we're focused on those we might be able to save for now."

"Aye, sir," Wallings answered. "I'll have my men two to a stretcher and bring in whomever they can. I'm afraid we're due back for dress parade shortly, but we'll do everything we can in the meantime."

"Any help is greatly appreciated."

Without further discussion, the men from the 49th went to work. Charley was paired with Alfred, and together they began to carry wounded to the operating areas. Getting the men on stretchers was difficult. Alfred would have to rock them up on their sides as carefully as possible while Charley pushed the stretcher under them. Once they were at least partially on, Alfred would roll them back and they would gently push the wounded the rest of the way.

Carrying them was not as difficult as Charley expected. Most were rather light, even for a boy of his size. Though, all the training he had undergone over the past several months had greatly increased his own strength. It had not occurred to him until that moment, but he realized then he was developing muscles where he never before knew he had any.

"Can I ask you something?" Alfred asked, interrupting Charley's thoughts.

"Sure," Charley said. "Is something wrong?"

"Not at all," Alfred replied. "I suppose I was just wondering how you were holding up after the first battle. It was more chaotic than I ever expected. I'm certain my hands did not stop shaking until the morning."

"Oh, I'm not sure. I guess I don't really remember," Charley admitted. "I remember hearing orders, and drumming out the cadences, but I... I suppose that's really all."

"I can understand that," Alfred said. "With all the smoke from the muskets, the noise and everything going on, it's hard to remember exactly what happened. I'm not sure how many times I fired my weapon. I certainly couldn't tell you if I hit anyone."

"The battle was won, regardless," Charley said. "You'll think I lie, but I wasn't scared at all. Nervous, perhaps. And overwhelmed with the noise and smoke, but not afraid. I suppose that's odd."

"I don't think so," Alfred replied. "In such a time, your body will implore you to do one of two things—either run or stand bravely. We have already seen the men who run. Your inclination is for the best in battle."

"Brave? I don't know about that."

"Well, not cowardly, at least," Alfred said.

As they reached the hospital tent, they found an open spot to place the wounded Confederate soldier they were carrying. They set him on the ground and gently rolled him off the stretcher and onto another sheet. He began to stir as they did so, and a moment later his eyes snapped open and he started to violently flail his arms.

"Hold on, hold on," Alfred said, trying to pin the man's arms down.

"Off, off, damned Yankees are everywhere… every…"

The Rebel locked eyes on Alfred, and then looked down at his blue uniform. Once it registered that he was in Federal hands, he began to struggle all the more. He tried to stand but his wound caused him to tumble back to the ground and cry out.

"Stifle that," Alfred hissed. "You're not going anywhere, but if you're lucky we might be able to save your life. I'll get the medic."

"Piss on your medic," the Rebel growled.

"What are you, stupid?" Charley shot back. "We're trying to save your rotten life. Have a little gratitude."

The Rebel looked over at Charley for a moment, then back at Alfred.

"Is this a damned hospital or a schoolhouse? What's this child doing in uniform? Lost to an army of little boys, dear Lord. You Yanks got women in your outfit, too? Suppose you'll be arming them slaves soon, too. Why don't ya sing us one of those old spirituals to ease our pain since yer clearly so in love with them lousy negroes."

Charley felt his face flush, and had Alfred not stood up and taken his arm, he might have attacked the man.

"It's a helluva lot easier to love them than it is the likes of you," Alfred muttered. "I think we're done with this fella. Let's see about a duty a little less indulging of foolishness."

"Yeah, run on Yankee bastards," the Rebel said as they walked away. Alfred shook his head. Charley was still too angry to speak, but before they could travel more than a few steps, another Rebel caught Alfred by the leg.

"Leave off," Alfred growled. "Someone will be along for you shortly."

"Wait," the other Rebel said, "that one there, we're not all like him. We don't all feel… it's about the cause for most of us."

Alfred looked down at the Rebel and wrinkled his nose in disgust.

"Cause. What cause?"

"Our rights," the Rebel replied, seeming baffled. "What did you all think this was about?"

"Owning folks," Alfred growled.

The Rebel gritted his teeth.

"Well, I never owned no one," he said, "but I don't see it as you or your president's place to tell us we can't live as we've lived for a hundred years."

"Then you're all like him," Alfred cut in. "Quit your excuses and accept the truth. I hope some negro has the pleasure of rolling your stinking corpse into your grave."

The Rebel and Charley alike were left speechless as Alfred trudged away. Charley hurried after him, trying his best to match his long strides, but it was clear Alfred was in no mood for further conversation. After a short distance, it was clear to Charley they were headed back to camp. On the way, though, they passed by the site of another skirmish they had not taken part in. When they arrived in the open field, they quickly realized that their fellow Northerners had not prevailed in this particular area.

Union soldiers lay dead, dotting the field. Charley looked down on one man, little older than himself, and felt his stomach turn. The Rebels had stripped him of his uniform and boots, as well as all of his ammunition. Chuck was right—both sides were guilty of robbing the dead. This realization did not comfort Charley in the least.

"What are these men still doing here?" Charley asked, looking across the field at the dead.

"I suppose gathering those killed was not as high a priority as rounding up the enemy's wounded."

"How long will they be left here?"

"I can't say," Alfred replied. "Likely, local citizens will be along in the days following our departure and will bury the dead. Some will end up in a mass grave. I suppose any officers found dead will be given grave markers. I'm not certain the same can be said for those like you and me."

Charley shook his head, saddened by the thought of his fellow soldiers lying forever unknown in some unmarked grave. How many would lie side by side with the men they stood beside? Was there some comfort in the knowledge that, though they lay without honor, they were surrounded by fellow soldiers?

Charley could not say.

They moved on from the battlefield, continuing to their camp where those who were not at the hospital were gathering Rebel weapons and ammunition. They made a large pile on the edge of camp and began preparing the spoils for transport. As they did so, Charley saw a long vanguard approaching in the distance with the flag of the Union fluttering overhead. A moment later, there came a call to fall in and Charley and Alfred hurried to do so. Most of their company being absent, they fell in with the members of Company D who stayed behind.

Standing at attention, they watched the vanguard approach until it stopped just before them. Col. Irwin stepped forward and saluted a man on horseback who bore the insignia of a general. The general saluted back and swung down off his horse.

"The battle was well fought," the general said. "You should be very proud of your men, Col. Irwin. Please make sure all your captains hear of my commendation."

"Thank you, General McClellan," Irwin replied. "I will be sure to relay your gratitude. These are the munitions we were able to capture from the Rebels. We hope they will serve your Army well."

"I'm certain they will," General McClellan said. "I cannot be more pleased with the way this battle played out. I am riding around to many regiments to tell them how well they have done. For now, carry on. It will likely not be long before we are in battle once again."

The men exchanged a salute, and General McClellan rode off to continue reviewing the troops. When he was gone, Col. Irwin gave the order to fall out, and the men went back about their business. Shortly after, the rest of Company F returned from hospital duty, looking weary and ready for rest. Alfred and Charley offered to find them dinner, as they had departed earlier than the others. There was some thought to making a fire, but the day had grown so hot that the idea seemed somewhat mad. They would, instead, seek provisions that did not require cooking.

They returned to find their friends in the company sitting in a circle as they often did. Chuck seemed calmer than he had earlier and gladly accepted a plate of beans from Charley.

"What led you two to abandon our duty so early?" he asked.

"My apologies for that," Alfred replied. "I grew hot at the words of a wounded Rebel. I thought Charley and I might abuse the man if we were to remain any longer. Truly, I would have liked to stay and rough him up, but I thought it best not to involve young Charley in my own sins."

"I see," Chuck replied, pausing a moment as a cough overtook him. "What did he say to you?"

"Excuses. Excuses decent men have no need to listen to," Alfred said. "It was clear to me that Charley did not care for them either. I suppose we were simply raised in a more civilized town than that wounded rat."

"Go on then," Abel put in, oddly interested in the conversation. "What exactly did the man say that boiled yer blood so?"

Alfred could not seem to bring himself to say the word, but it had bothered Charley so that he felt compelled to voice it.

"He had the gall to defend their war because of their *rights*. Rights to own a man. And he used some words I don't think are right," he said. "At least, that's what upset me."

Abel frowned.

"That's it? Hell, can't be upset with him for *that*."

Chuck looked as though he might clap Abel across the head, but he restrained himself. Instead, he shot a hard stare at him.

"He don't like it," Chuck replied, "that's what's wrong."

"You cannot be serious," Abel shot back.

"My father told me a man is a man," Joe offered. "He said no matter what ya think of black folk, they're men same as us."

"Oh hell," Abel muttered. "John Brown hisself done rose from the grave to give me a lecture on who's a man and what to call him."

"Why are you even here?" Chuck growled. "Why put on that uniform?"

"Don't you give a damn about freedom?" Charley added.

"Freedom?" Abel scoffed. "I give a damn about *my* freedom. That's what the Constitution promised me and I'll be damned if some Southern rats are gonna spit in the face of that. Don't tell me you're all here for the negroes?"

"Of course," Alfred replied, taken aback.

"Well," John Coon put in, "I certainly don't think slavery is *right* but, I have to agree with Abel. This is *one* country and I believe God wants it to be so. The slaves, well…"

"We ought to be here for both," Chuck put in. "If you ask me, anyway."

Abel shrugged.

"Don't seem to me that you get a say why any of us are here. Not you, not Alfred, not Lincoln himself. If I thought the only reason to be here was to fight for some negroes, I'd turn tail and head home in a minute."

With that, Abel got up and stalked away, shaking his head as he went.

"I'd rather fight beside a dozen negroes than a single Abel Tyson," Alfred said, turning his attention back to his food.

"Aye," Chuck agreed. "It's a pity some good men died and a man like him lives on. I suppose that's too often the way of it."

"I wouldn't wish any more death than we've already seen," John Coon put in. "No matter what kind of man he is."

Chuck shook his head.

"John, boy, you must be the only man in the North *or* South who cares a wit for Abel Tyson." As he finished, he launched into another coughing fit, and Charley could see concern begin to grow in Alfred's face.

"Maybe," John shrugged, ignoring the cough. "Maybe I've just seen enough death."

"Well, that ain't up to you," Chuck replied, after catching his breath. "That's up to Mr. Lincoln, Mr. Davis, and the Lord God Almighty."

CHAPTER 12

Seven Days Battles

Charley had experienced the intense heat of August in West Chester, but nothing could prepare him for Virginia's June. Perhaps it was the constant march with no resolution or the boredom that came with long stays in camp, but it seemed to him that late spring days in the South were near twice as long as they were in Pennsylvania. And twice as hot, as well.

Charley soldiered on without complaint as best he could. There wasn't much he could do about a single thing, anyway. The workings of the Army of the Potomac were far beyond him. He even heard they had been reassigned to the Sixth Corps, though the ramifications of that reassignment seemed to be negligible. They remained under General Hancock, so what did it matter?

The rest of his company kept their chins up for the most part, aside from a few instances of mild vitriol mostly aimed at Colonel Irwin. One day in particular the boys were pretty riled up. Col. Irwin had refused to let them have any crackers on account of the fact they, according to the colonel, were not "wholesome." Charley was not terribly certain what he meant by that, but he did not care much for the crackers anyhow. Others apparently liked them quite a bit, because Charley heard one soldier remark that he would sooner shoot Irwin that night than a Rebel.

That was just idle talk, Charley was fairly certain, but there was a fair amount of dissent in the ranks over that particular decision. It did not help that the going was rather rough and while there was talk of clashes with the Rebels around the area, they did not face any battles themselves.

Then came Friday, June 27.

It was already near unbearably hot as the regiment stood in line at 3:30 in the morning. They'd had what would have to pass for breakfast in the dark of night before marching out to the picket line to support the workmen digging rifle pits. Word had gone around that the Rebels were headed their way and would be within range to attack by around 9 am. The 49th took up a position at the edge of a nearby wood where the enemy would not be able to see them upon approach.

Charley stood hunched by the brush with his drumsticks tucked into his waistband. Joe was beside him, nervously thumbing at his fife while the rest of the company checked their weapons in preparation for the coming fight. A handful of men from their regiment, about 36, including Alfred Moulder, had detached from the rest and marched up a nearby hill about 100 yards back. There was stationed the First Connecticut Artillery with four 32-pounders trained on the path of the Rebels' most likely approach.

Not long before noon, the regiment still lay in wait for the Confederate approach and were beginning to grow antsy.

"I thought they were to be along by nine," Joe muttered. "Don't they know there's a battle to be fought?"

Chuck could not help but laugh.

"Suppose my old sweetheart from back home must be leading them," he said, "seeing as the boys are nigh on three hours late."

"I imagine she always showed up for the likes of you, though, eh?" Joe shot back with a smile.

"Aye," Chuck nodded, "she always showed. Reckon the Rebel boys will show, too."

The conversation had not passed five minutes when the sound of ten Rebel 12-pounders tore the sky. Shells burst overhead and rained down shrapnel, causing several men to dive behind the trees for cover. A moment later, the 2nd Connecticut returned fire, peppering the enemy with shells. The batteries lobbed ordinance back and forth as the men of the 49th hunkered down in between.

Charley watched as a shell found the line near Company D and sent a fair many men tumbling through the air. The blast jostled him such that he nearly tumbled over, despite the several dozen yards between his position and where the shell landed. As he steadied himself, he saw Lt. Wallings cast a glance in his direction and the memory of the Rebel ship outside Newport News flashed back into his mind. Wallings had been right—that shelling was child's play.

Charley had no idea if a similar thought had crossed the lieutenant's mind, but another exploding shell brought the moment to a quick end. Two men nearby began to fall back, making as if to flee. In a moment, Lt. Wallings had them both by one arm each and yanked them back down to the ground.

"Hold the line, yeh nitwits," he shouted. "I don't care if you're damned cowards. You'll fight and if yeh try to flee you'll only die quicker."

There was no doubt in Charley's mind, or the minds of the would-be deserters, that the lieutenant's threat was genuine. They fell back into place and clutched their weapons close to their chests. Not minutes later, riding up the back of the line came Gen. Hancock with his orderly in close pursuit.

"Good on yeh, men," Hancock shouted. "Hold the line and keep your heads down. We'll have that battery off the hill in no time and after that we'll have 'em weakened. They won't know what to do, boys!"

The regiment cheered at Hancock's proclamation, but his orderly seemed none-too-thrilled.

"General," he said, "hadn't we better get out of this?"

Hancock looked down his nose at the orderly with heavy disdain.

"No, we ain't any better than those men lying there."

The orderly frowned, but the statement only fired up the boys even more. Hancock paid him no further mind and beckoned for Col. Irwin to come forward. Irwin hurried over, head bent as the shells continued to explode overhead.

"Listen Colonel," Hancock said, "when this barrage has ended, I want you to take your men and make for that small stream over yonder. About ten feet from that position there's a long ditch that'll be a safer spot should things grow any hotter. Do you understand?"

"Aye, sir," Irwin said. "First lull we have in the volley I'll rally the men to that position."

Hancock nodded and rode off with his orderly still huffing and puffing close behind. Soon after, the cannonading stopped and Captain Sweney immediately gave the order for Company F to make for the ditch. The whole of the 49th Regiment followed hurriedly, seeking safe refuge before the battle started up again. They fell into the ditch with a great number of relieved sighs, before turning to face the field.

"I can't see why we didn't make our line here in the first place," Joe said as he peeked out from the ditch. "Seems far safer."

"Most likely the general expected an infantry attack," Lt. Wallings said, "so he had us somewhere we could meet it more effectively. More importantly, it was an order and we follow orders."

"Right," Joe said, clearly not satisfied with the answer. Truly, however, there was no other answer, Charley reasoned. Any question of why an action was taken ought best be handled by an officer and not expressed by a private.

They lay in the ditch, as ordered, until around nightfall, when the Rebels opened fire once more with cannon. This attack, however, was short lived. Wallings kept his head above the edge of the ditch as the attack went on and, after a few minutes, called out to Captain Sweney.

"There's a heavy body of infantry to our front, sir. Looks like they're moving to stay between us and Richmond. I'll warrant they'll be on our skirmishers in no time at all. Someone ought to alert Colonel Irwin."

"I'm already aware, Lieutenant," Irwin called from just behind the line. "You form up, boys. Charley, strike the long roll and let's show these Rebs what for!"

It quickly became apparent that this was General Hancock's plan when he first sent the 49th back to the ditch. As they formed into ranks and took up their position, the Rebels spotted them and wheeled in their direction. With a chorus of harsh cries, the enemy charged their position. A moment later, they were met with a sheet of fire from end to end, flashing brightly in the darkness. Charley noted that the cries of the Rebel attackers were not so loud after that.

They continued on, advancing boldly toward the line with such aggression that Charley wondered for a moment if the 49th could hold. He never truly got the chance to find out, however. As the hornets buzzed overhead, Charley heard the familiar sound of marching orders tapped out from their flank. He wheeled around and could just make out another regiment of Union boys approaching the battlefield, muskets at the ready. Taking quick note of the Rebel advance, it was clear that they were not yet aware of the approaching regiment and that their cries and musket fire deafened them to the marching cadence.

Charley gave another excited glance toward their fellow Federal troops as Captain Sweney hustled by.

"Reinforcements!" Charley shouted to him as he ran.

"Aye," Sweney called back, "the 4th Vermont! Never thought I'd be so glad to see them Green Mountain Boys!"

Not long after, the Rebels began to realize their change in fortunes. Before they could wheel about to meet the 4th Vermont, a barrage of leaden pellets swept across the field and cut down several dozen of their men. Now knowing themselves to be routed, the Rebels turned tail and fled across the field into a nearby ravine. The 49th Pennsylvania and 4th Vermont pursued them only a little further to make certain they did not reform. Once they were confident that the Rebels had truly fled, both regiments removed their caps to one another and cheered.

The celebration was short, however, as they were ordered back to their camps right away. It was 9 pm by the time the 49th returned to their tents and not a man among them was not bone-weary and sore from the day's escapades. Charley was barely awake enough to make it to his bedroll before collapsing and falling into a deep sleep.

The sound of musket fire ripped Charley from his sleep early the next morning. He could not guess how long he had been asleep, but the camp was alive with activity. Captains were shouting out orders, and Charley stumbled out of his tent with his drum strapped on in time to hear the duties of the day.

The captains of companies C, D, I, and A were calling their men together to march for the Chickahominy River, which stood to the right of a nearby Confederate fort. Uncertain what that meant for his own company, Charley frantically searched the area for Captain Sweney. The man was nowhere to be found but his own regiment seemed unconcerned.

The only officer nearby was Lt. Wallings, who saw Charley looking frantic and approached him.

"This is quite the wild scramble, eh?" he said, offering a rare moment of levity. "Too bad they don't need another company. The poor boys of F hate to be bored."

"I suppose," Charley replied. "Where is Captain Sweney? Do we have any orders at all or are they just sending out the four companies?"

"We'll be forming up reserves, I expect," Wallings said. "I wouldn't worry too much about the captain. He'll be around soon enough. Likely, he's with Col. Irwin plannin' the advance or something of the like. You worry about being prepared for whatever the next order is. I'll worry about anything else."

Charley nodded, though not feeling terribly satisfied with the response. Once his tent was in order, he simply found a seat with the other soldiers and waited as the day progressed. By late morning, news started trickling in of the day's engagements. Around 9 am, the four companies and the 43rd New York had taken fire by the Chickahominy. They only lost one man when the Rebels charged the position. The Union boys pushed them back, causing heavy losses amongst the Confederate ranks and taking a number of prisoners.

Early in the afternoon, word went around that the companies were returning and that the regiment was to make a line to cover their retreat. The rest of the 49th was on the task immediately, forming up and hurrying to the nearby woods as their boys returned. They met one another at the woods and allowed the companies who had gone out to skirmish to fall in behind them and take their rest.

The Rebels, for their part, seemed to have gotten their fill and turned about to return to their own lines. As they did, a round of laughter could be heard from behind and Charley turned to see some of the men from Company H standing over an injured soldier. He was an older man and was clearly out of breath and bloody.

"Tell it again, Robbins," someone said to him, "the rest of the boys haven't heard it."

"Oh they don't care about all that," the old man replied.

"Don't care about what?" Alfred shouted. "Let's hear it, Robbins. What's warranted all the laughter?"

"Old Joe almost got caught," another man from H said. "Go on, Joe."

"Alright," Robbins said. "We were headed off the skirmish line and I had to grab my knapsack. I suppose that slowed me down a bit because the next thing I hear is some damned Rebels telling me to surrender. So I says, 'surrender hell!' and kept on headed toward the line. Well, not a minute later them boys are yellin' for me to surrender or they'll shoot, so naturally I shouted 'shoot and be damned,' and kept on going."

"So what did they do?" Alfred asked.

"What do you think?" Robbins replied, "the Rebs shot me."

A roar of laughter followed the end of the story and Charley shook his head in admiration. He should have liked to know how Joe Robbins escaped, but he was already being carried back to the camp. Instead, he hunkered down with the rest and they remained in the rifle pits until 6 pm when the entire brigade came together once more and formed a line. There was still musket fire in the distance and Charley wondered if it meant the day was not yet done.

"Where do you think those shots are coming from?" he asked. Chuck Butler leered into the distance, trying to formulate his best guess.

"There was a spot back behind the lines a bit called Savage Station. It might be over that way. Or it could be closer to White House Landing. Either way, it's behind the lines. I don't like the meaning generally accompanied by that. If Johnny Reb's circled behind us, you can bet we'll be headed that way soon enough."

"Aye, so get some rest," Lt. Wallings said. "Might be tomorrow noon, might be tomorrow before first light. There's Rebels on two, maybe three sides of us. We ain't leavin' here without one hell of a fight."

CHAPTER 13

Savage Station and White Oak Swamp

Both men proved to be correct in their estimations. By early the next morning, the 49th was on the move toward Savage Station. Charley was not certain if he had slept during the night or not, but if he had it was for a bare few minutes. Those around him must have had much the same experience, as the entire regiment looked bleary-eyed and heavily fatigued. Not a one complained, though, not even Abel. The entirety of the 49th moved in relative silence, their heavy footsteps the only sound beside the constant beating of the marching cadence.

They moved along through most of the day with Charley drumming the cadence. He paused only a few times to rest his hands, but each time he did, another cadence could be heard not far from them.

"Johnny Reb is close behind," Lt. Wallings said. "Hopefully we find a good position before he catches us."

The sun above them was unforgiving, bearing down on them like the heat of a roaring bonfire. Sweat soaked through Charley's undershirt and began to darken the blue of his uniform. Beside him, he could see that Joe, too, was wearing down from the heat. All along the lines, men were emptying their canteens and finding nothing with which to refill them. Charley, too, was running low and the sun still hung high in the sky.

"Are we going to get more water soon?" he asked Joe, who shrugged with a frown.

"I haven't seen a cart nor a well all day," he said. "If water is on its way, I cannot guess where it might be coming from."

"I'm near out," Charley grumbled. "It's pretty clear the rest of the regiment is running low, as well. Do they expect us to fight when we can hardly stand?"

"I think they would expect us to fight if we had one leg and no eyes," Joe chuckled. "Anyway, there's no use complaining about it. If there's water to be found, Col. Irwin will make sure we get some."

"Your 'if' is not terribly comforting," Charley replied. Joe simply shrugged and they fell back into silence.

THE BATTLE OF SAVAGE'S STATION. FROM A SKETCH MADE AT THE TIME.

The battle of Savage's Station was part of the Seven Days Battles, a series of clashes which ultimately led to the Union Army's withdrawal and the end of the Peninsula Campaign. During these battles, Robert E. Lee, who had become commander of Confederate forces just weeks earlier, repelled the Union advance and pushed them back to Harrison's Landing. (Clarence Buel and Robert Johnson, eds., *Battles and Leaders of the Civil War, being for the most part contributions by Union and Confederate Soldiers* (New York: The Century Company, 1887), 394)

Charley's hands were growing tired by the time the regiment reached the York River Railroad. Col. Irwin ordered them to fall into a line on the right side of the railroad, between the station and the bridge. Joe and Charley moved toward the back of the line as they took up their position, rifles in hand. There were a few urgent whispers, but for the most part the line remained quiet.

As the day drew on, it became clear that there must not have been water to find. The sun sank lower, but the heat did not break and the 49th Regiment grew more and more thirsty. There was little to do about it besides wait and hope that water would come.

Instead, the Rebels came.

Just before sundown, a line of Rebel soldiers appeared and the 49th hunkered down in preparation. They moved swiftly toward the station, such that there could be no question of their intention. Charley beat out the long roll, on the off chance anyone on the line was not already formed up and ready. Across the field, the Rebels were moving quickly, crying out as they did in the earlier battles. The 49th, for their part, stood well behind the front line.

Company F watched from afar as the skirmish began, but part of their regiment was engaged in the fighting. Charley was not certain which companies, but he could see several of the officers preparing for battle. Colonel Irwin was shouting out orders as the Rebels approach, but it was Major Hulings who caught Charley's eye. He stood among the men with his revolver drawn and his face the picture of calm. While the men around him raised their weapons, many of their hands were visibly shaking, but Hulings stood firm.

A moment later, a torrent of fire and smoke erupted from the line and peppered the Rebels with a cloud of bullets. Charley watched about a dozen men fall to their knees and crash to the earth as their fellow soldiers continued on. Another volley cut through the Rebel line moments later, and they began to pick up speed. Some lowered their weapons and fired into the line, with several shots hitting the mark. The Union boys stood bravely, though, returning fire with a great ferocity.

Charley watched as Major Hulings coolly took aim, making sure every shot counted. A man fell beside him, but he did not so much as flinch.

He fired until his revolver emptied and then began to reload. Bullet after bullet, he calmly loaded the weapon and then commenced firing once more. His poise was like something out of a newspaper story or one of the dime novels Charley and his friends use to read. Frightened as he was, Charley could not help but be inspired.

Keeping his head down, he watched between the shoulders of two of his fellow Pennsylvanians as the Rebels press forward. Volley after volley and the Rebels kept advancing, somehow undeterred by the rain of bullets. For a moment, Charley marveled at their bravery, wondering if he would have the courage to march so boldly toward death. But the marvel did not last. Brave as the Rebels were, the staunchly held Union position proved too much for them. Before they could reach the line, they were repulsed. They fell back and took up their own position, firing upon the regiment from across the field.

The enemy now concentrated in a uniform line, their musket volleys became more regular and inflicted greater injury upon the Union line. Charley heard the bullets whizzing through the air and ducked a little lower, doing his best to keep the enemy in view. He wanted to see what was happening, but he knew Captain Sweney would be upset if he allowed himself to be injured. Still, he could not help but watch.

After an hour of exchanging fire, the Rebels turned tail and left the field. The fight ended rather abruptly, and the retreat was followed by several moments of silence. A few men began to cheer half-heartedly, but most simply lowered their weapons and searched around for their canteens. Those that had water shared what little was left and most just had to go without. It was an unfortunate state of affairs, but there was nothing much for it. Supplies were thin and there was no changing that.

After a short rest, the men fell in again—all except for Chuck, who Charley saw was sitting propped against the side of a ditch, his face pale. His heart leaping into his throat, Charley hurried over to him, followed closely by Joe and Alfred. When he was nearly there, Chuck turned, and Charley felt relief wash over him. He was alive, but he looked much worse for wear.

"Were you hit?" Charley asked. "Are you alright?"

Chuck shook his head weakly and said,

"Hit? No. We weren't even… yeah, I'm alright."

"You don't look alright," Alfred replied. "You've been looking worse every passing day since all the rain by Williamsburg. You ought to maybe consider heading to the infirmary."

"Piss on that," Chuck muttered, but he could not muster any further words. As he lay there, Captain Sweney rode up and looked down from his horse.

"You're ill, soldier," the captain said. "You shouldn't be on the line."

"Hell, Captain," Chuck replied with a cough. "I wasn't about to miss my chance to fight for nothin'."

"Well, the engagement is over," Sweney said. "We're like to be in battle again soon and I can't have a sick man slowing down the march. You'll be staying here for now until the medical corps can come tend to you. We'll see if we can't break through the Rebel lines and then we'll all meet back up when you're well. For now, you've seen enough action. Go on."

Chuck knew better than to protest. With the help of Alfred and Joe, he made his way to a shady spot where he could rest. Once he was off, Captain Sweney turned to the rest of the company, still atop his horse.

"We're headed toward James River," he said, "but there's a good amount of damn fine supplies here. Unfortunately, we ain't in any position to take it along, but we're not about to leave it for Johnny Reb. Destroy anything you see and make sure it can't be used a lick, understand?"

"Aye, sir," the company called back.

"Alright, we march once it's fully dark," Sweney continued. "Get to it."

Capt. Sweney rode away without another word. Lt. Wallings stood forward as he hurried off and gave a wave to the men.

"You heard the captain. Smash it all to bits!"

Worried as they were about Chuck, the company got a fair amount of pleasure out of smashing up the remaining supplies. John, in particular, savagely ravaged the packages of food they could not carry along. Charley could see the tension growing behind his eyes and it was clear the release was needed. Alfred was less enthusiastic about smashing things—his thoughts were on Chuck and his illness. Abel Tyson did not even bother to participate, instead waiting in the shade for the sun to finally vanish behind the horizon.

For their part, Charley and Joe smashed up a few crates, but only destroyed enough to demonstrate their participation in the captain's orders. Lt. Wallings did not seem overly concerned about who was doing the most to destroy the supplies, so long as everything was smashed beyond salvaging by the time they left—and it most certainly was.

Once dark had overcome the station and the captured Rebel supplies had been reduced to ruins, Col. Irwin gave the order to march and the whole regiment fell in. They marched on through the darkness away from the station until they reached James River around midnight. Once there, they crossed over into the White Oak Swamp and found a hillside to camp on. A great many men stopped to fill their canteens at the river and Charley did not think he had ever felt such a wave of relief as when that cool water first touched his lips.

Nearly equal to that relief was that which came when he fell into his bedroll and plunged into a deep sleep. He could not say later if he had dreamed. If he had, there was no time to dwell on what visions flashed through his unconscious mind. Whatever he had seen in sleep was wholly obliterated by the crashing of artillery shells that dragged him into wakefulness the following morning.

Captain Sweney was ordering men down to the base of the hill when Charley wrenched himself upright. The world around him was a cacophony of shattering shells, billowing smoke, and dirt raining down from all sides. There was nothing for it but to run for shelter and he found himself tumbling down the hill, his drum rolling after him. He slid to a stop and caught the instrument before climbing into a ditch at the base of the hill. Alfred was beside him a moment later, musket in hand.

"They're shelling the damned horses," he said, his heavy breath weighing down his words. "In half a damned minute they cut the lot of them down. Looks like the captain is going to have tired legs tonight."

"Let's hope we all *have* legs tonight," John shouted from a few feet away.

"Well, we sure as hell ain't walkin' in this," Alfred roared, "legs or no."

A moment later, Captain Sweney slid into the ditch beside them.

"Rebel bastards killed my horse," he growled. "Who kills a horse? That's downright ungentlemanly."

"Aye, I was saying just that not a moment ago," Alfred replied, casting a sly smile toward Charley, who chuckled.

"Well I'm glad you're entertained, Mr. King," Captain Sweney said. "As for me, I'm at a loss. How are we going to get orders if the men are running all over the place and can't ride? This is a damned mess, that's what it is."

"My guess," Alfred offered, "if you don't mind my sayin' sir, is that we ain't going anywhere in this little storm and ought to stay hunkered down in this here ditch until things clear up. That, of course, is up to you, sir."

"Like hell it's up to me," Sweney grumbled. "If General Hancock says it's time to move, it's time to move. I imagine we'd lose half the regiment if we tried to slip on out of here, though. Suppose that would teach him a thing or two."

"You don't think he would, do you?" Charley asked as another round of shells crashed into the hillside.

"Don't rightly know," Sweney confessed. "If Hancock has his way, we'll likely make some kind of charge toward the enemy line. Should McClellan fancy giving an order, though, we'll probably wait until victory is at hand and then turn tail and run."

Charley frowned.

"I never guessed you all didn't agree on what was best. Do the officers disagree a lot?"

Captain Sweney replied with a grim laugh.

"You could say it happens from time to time, but you didn't hear that from me. Don't matter worth a lick anyway. Old Colonel Irwin's about as tired of it as anyone. Doesn't mean we ain't gonna follow whatever orders come down—even if it means we stand on the hill wavin' our arms about and singin' how we wish we were in Dixie."

Charley was thankful to find it did not come to that. Instead, they stayed put until night fell again, at which time Col. Irwin gave the order to withdraw from their position. All the horses were dead, so the colonel, the captain, and all the lieutenants trudged along beside the rest of the soldiers. They continued on throughout the night as cannon fire continued in the distance. The Rebels, it seemed, were determined not to let a man in Virginia get a good night's rest.

With the dawn came new orders, as well as the return of oppressive summer heat. July had arrived and Virginia would not let the Union boys forget it. Charley thought of the boys from the 4th Vermont and wondered if they were withering in this weather. All he knew of Vermont were the heavy snows that covered the Green Mountains and, if he remembered correctly, how it stayed a fine brisk temperature through most of the year. Anyone used to that weather must be near to death in this.

The 49th was ordered to support a nearby artillery regiment, which was continuously raining ordinance on the Rebels as they moved about. Charley was somewhat relieved to find they were a fair distance from the front line and, though the men remained on high alert, it was unlikely they would face the enemy that day.

Instead, the men of the 49th took their rest, eyes trained toward the front lines, but bodies at ease in the oppressive heat. They stayed there throughout the entire day, watching for any sign of the enemy and seeing none. Their vigil continued into the evening and overnight until, at 3 am, a messenger from General Hancock came hurrying up. He saluted Col. Irwin and handed him new orders. After taking a few moments to read over them, Irwin nodded and handed the paper back. His captains gathered around him as he relayed the orders. After a round of salutes, they returned to their companies.

"Listen up," Captain Sweney said, "new orders I think you're going to like. Our artillery has cleared the road and there's another regiment coming up to relieve us, boys. We're ordered to withdraw."

"Not back to the marsh, is it?" John grumbled, but Wallings silenced him with a cold stare.

"Not at all, Mr. Coon," the captain said, "we're withdrawing all the way back to Harrison's Landing."

The chorus of relieved sighs that followed rivaled the artillery battery in volume and the men immediately began to pack up their things. It had been over two months since they landed on the Virginia Peninsula and, while they had not seen constant action, the threat of battle had loomed over them with every passing minute.

Now, at long last, they would have real rest.

CHAPTER 14

Harrison's Landing

The journey back to Harrison's Landing was slow, and each mile felt like another unending dream. Rain had muddied both the road and the fields around it, so the sludge and filth ruled both their days and nights. The camp at the landing was no better than the fields on the way there. Not a single man wasn't caked in mud by the time they finally reached the end of their march.

The morning after their arrival, Charley finally had the energy to think of something other than where he would place his foot next. A malaise lay over the camp and the officers seemed wholly disinterested in rousing the men. Instead, they took their own rest as well, having been without horses for several days. Captain Sweney appeared sparingly, stopping only to check the men at reveille and before supper. He occasionally updated them on the goings on of the campaign, but usually only relayed their orders, which were fairly simple—stay put.

For most of the first two days, that meant laying flat on the ground to avoid ever being seen. Orders were that not a man was to raise up off the ground. Colonel Irwin stood on a hilltop looking down over the field before him, though there were some grumblings in the regiment that he was back on the hilltop so that he need not lay in the dirt. Still, that was his right as commander, and no one was going to say a thing about it.

As the evening neared, Charley heard some scrambling nearby and turned to see Lt. Wombacker shuffling his way toward Captain Sweney. When he reached the captain, he said,

"Do you know what I just realized, Captain?"

"That we've been lying in the dirt for nearly forty-eight hours, and I haven't seen a single movement out of the Rebels the entire time?" Sweney replied.

"No sir," Wombacker replied, then paused a moment. "Well, yes, sir. I had noticed that, too. But sir, it's the Fourth."

"It might feel like that lieutenant, but it's actually only the second day we've been here," Sweney grumbled.

"No sir, it's the Fourth of July," Wombacker said. "Independence Day, sir. And we haven't done a thing to celebrate."

Captain Sweney replied with a wry laugh.

"Wombacker, do me a favor," he said. "Stand up and look over at that Rebel line and tell me if it looks like they're celebrating."

"Really, sir?" Lt. Wombacker replied. "Is that a good idea?"

"Damned if I know," Sweney said. "But I just told you to do it, didn't I?"

Lt. Wombacker pursed his lips and then nodded. Pushing himself up, he peered out over the field toward the Rebel lines. Almost instantly, the company heard a roar from the hill behind them.

"Lieutenant Wombacker," came the cry from Colonel Irwin. "Consider yourself under arrest!"

Lt. Wombacker dropped to the ground like a broken tree limb. The soldiers around him were unsure whether to laugh or try to lie even flatter than before. After a moment, Lt. Wombacker looked over to Captain Sweney.

"Is he serious?" Wombacker asked.

"I'm not sure," Sweney replied. "But I doubt he'll remember tomorrow and you would have to stand up again to leave the line. So, I wouldn't worry about it. Now, what about those Rebels? Are they celebrating?"

"No, sir," Wombacker answered. "They're still as we are."

"Well, of course," Chuck called from a few yards away. "There ain't no such thing as Confederate Independence Day. Well, not if we have anything to say about it."

A roll of laughter rippled through the company. Even Lt. Wombacker smiled in spite of what had just transpired. After the laughter had died down though, he leaned in close to Captain Sweney once more.

"Why did you make me do that?" he asked.

"It's been a dull day, Frank. *Something* had to happen. And besides, they weren't going to shoot you when there's a colonel in plain sight."

Lt. Wombacker seemed to be satisfied by this answer and the entire company resumed lying in silence.

On the fourth day at Harrison's Landing, things had settled down and the regiment was free to move about some. At about midday, Alfred came walking into camp with a glowering look. He had left the day before to see about Chuck and his demeanor betrayed unfortunate news. Charley and Joe were sitting by their tents with Abel, John, and Lt. Wallings all seated nearby. When he arrived beside them, Alfred slumped down to sit in mud without a care for the dampness seeping into his trousers.

"Bad news?" Joe asked. "I suppose there ain't been such a thing as good news lately, has there."

Alfred shook his head.

"Typhoid fever," he said. "Camp fever, folks tend to call it. I suppose you all can imagine why."

"Hell," Abel muttered, "suppose it's a good thing he left when he did then, hey? No use draggin' the whole company into it."

"Abel, so help me," Joe growled, but Wallings raised a hand to quiet him.

"He's right, lout that he is," Wallings said. "Still, many men recover from typhoid. I reckon we may see Mr. Butler again soon enough."

"That'll be tough," Alfred replied, "seein' as he died two days ago."

"Lord Almighty," Wallings said, "a tough old dog like Butler taken down by Camp Fever? I don't believe it."

"Well, believe it," Alfred muttered. "They hadn't buried him yet when I got there. I watched them roll him into the ground, so I'm pretty damn confident he's dead."

"Oh hell," John cried, "oh hell, damnation. We're all gonna be in the bottom of a grave soon enough."

"Shut it," Wallings hissed. "If ya get sick, ya get sick and there ain't a damn thing to be done about it, so calm yourself."

Abel joined the argument, and tempers quickly began to run hot. Charley did not engage, but the others looked as though they might come to blows. So tense was the moment, that none but Charley noticed

Captain Sweney approaching. He rose to his feet and stood to attention, as the captain waited for the others to notice. When they didn't, he loudly cleared his throat, and the others whirled around with sheepish looks on their face.

"Butler?" Sweney asked.

"Dead," was all Alfred could muster. Captain Sweney nodded.

"I'm sorry, boys," he said. "I know a lot of you were close with him, but I'm afraid this is the way things go. Camp can be as dangerous a place as the battlefield sometimes. Just because a man walks away from musket fire, doesn't mean he'll walk away from a fever. You boys get some rest and make damn sure you tell someone the minute you feel ill."

The men all muttered "yes, sir" as Captain Sweney turned away and headed off. Wallings stood up and followed after him. The rest all sat down again, having lost the heart to fight with one another. How any could have let their blood run so hot in the first place was a marvel to Charley. For days at a time, they had been under the threat of battle, and they decided to fight while safe at camp. It seemed madder than a mangy old dog to him. Heat, he supposed, could do that to a person.

For now, however, everyone seemed to have lost their hunger for fighting. Instead, they resigned themselves to calm conversation.

"I don't know how much more I can take," John said. "The past few days have been unlike anything I've ever experienced. It's been something like the worst storm I've ever seen in my life, but sustained over two weeks. That doesn't even sound bad enough."

"There's nothing to compare it to," Joe said. "Bullets flying, cannons, and the smoke nearly choking you to death. I think hell is the closest comparison I can find."

"I'm not ready for hell," John replied.

"Then maybe you ought to take your safety into your own hands, boy," Abel said. "You don't want to die, then you're in the wrong place."

"Don't hassle the kid," Alfred told him.

"Maybe I want to hear what he has to say," John replied. Alfred just shrugged and rolled his eyes, as Abel scooted in closer.

"The way I see it," he whispered, "you ain't leavin' this army if they have anything to say about it, unless it's in a box or into a grave. If you want to survive this war, you had better take action. And don't think for a minute about what people might call you. There ain't nothin' cowardly about saving your own life."

"Abel," Alfred cut in, "you are not seriously suggesting the boy desert, are you? He'll be caught before he crosses the picket line."

"The pickets don't care," Abel shot back. "They don't want to be here any more than young John does. They're more likely to be jealous of him than they are to try and stop him. I could say the same for every man in this regiment."

"The hell you can," Charley growled, surprising Abel with his anger. "You're the only one not man enough to stand and fight. Maybe you should desert."

"Aye, real easy to be brave from the back," Abel said in a mocking voice. "I wouldn't expect any less from Captain Sweney's dog."

"Move along, Abel," Alfred replied. "You've worn out your welcome, by several weeks."

Abel huffed and stood up, headed away to his own business. When he was gone, Alfred turned toward John and leaned in toward him.

"Fear is natural, but we are here for a reason," he said.

"Are we?" John replied. "I don't know that I ever even met a black fella. And I'm here risking my life for all of them? I'm not sure that's worth it to me."

"It's not just about black men," Joe offered, "though for some of us it is. But this is our nation, John. We're fighting to hold it together."

"Aye," Alfred said, "Some odd generations ago part of my family came from the foot of the Swiss Alps. Some folks came from Wales. But hell, my father was born in America, and I was sure as hell born in America. That makes me a damned American, and it makes you one, too. I ain't never heard of no country called Germany, anyhow. Charley, you an American?"

"As sure as I sit here."

"Joe?"

"That's the flag I march under," Joe replied, stifling a cough. "That makes me an American as far as I'm concerned."

"So I suppose them mick boys out of Philadelphia are Americans in your eyes?" John said. "Even though their blood's greener than a field of clover?"

"They spill that blood along the same line as we do?" Alfred asked. John didn't answer, but there was no need to do so. At least in this company, he was outnumbered.

"Well, thank the Lord you all aren't running the country," John finally said. "You'd probably have micks in the White House and Negroes voting, ya loons. I sure hope Mr. Lincoln ain't as daft as you all."

Without further discussion, John rose to his feet and stalked off in much the same way Abel had, leaving Charley, Alfred, and Joe alone. When he was out of earshot, Charley turned to the other two.

"You know, I never expected to find anyone in the army who didn't at least think black folks ought not be slaves," he said.

"I can't say I'm surprised," Alfred replied. "Some do it for the pay. Some people fight because they think this country is worth keeping together. Other people sign up because everyone in town is off to war. No matter the reason a man fights, a lot can change when he faces down a loaded weapon, I suppose. That's why they say war tests a man's mettle. You can stand for whatever you want to, but it's how you respond when another man is willing to shoot you for that stand.

"A man that runs from battle probably wasn't there for the right reasons to start with."

"I suppose not," Charley replied. "Have you felt at all like running?"

"Hell no," Alfred laughed. "A Moulder don't go anywhere without a purpose. And when a Moulder finds a purpose, you can bet he ain't givin' up until he's dead or it's done. Don't let anyone tell you any differently."

"I sure won't," Charley said.

"Good, now get some rest, both of you," Alfred replied. "You especially, Joe. You don't look so good."

Joe smiled, though his fatigue was clear as day.

"I'm fine," he said. "Don't you worry about me."

CHAPTER 15

Disease

Alfred, it turned out, was right to be worried about Joe. As it happened, he ought to be worried about himself, too. In fact, by mid-July, half the regiment had fallen ill. So widespread was the sickness that there were scarcely enough men left to drill. Those who were healthy were left to dig new latrines at an ungodly rate. Soldiers could barely keep their food down, and what they were able to keep in their stomachs came out in as unpleasant a manner as possible on the other end.

Charley was lucky enough to stay healthy and found himself pulling extra duties alongside Lt. Wallings. The rash of sickness concerned him greatly, and the increase in work helped him to keep his mind off those suffering around him. He even worked picket one day, though there were no Rebels to be seen for miles around. For the time being, Harrison's Landing was a safe place. Charley realized that was likely the reason Captain Sweney had allowed him to go out, but he was glad of the distraction.

The day he was on picket, he returned to camp quite weary from the long watch. The camp was quiet as it often was, with only the sound of a few soft groans from the ill soldiers. Many had been taken to the infirmary, but those who were not quite in dire straits remained in their tents. Charley stopped first by Alfred's tent and peered in, but Alfred was fast asleep, so he continued on.

Next he came to Joe's tent and looked inside to find him writhing in pain. His skin was a ghastly white and he was drooling heavily. Charley rushed in and tried to speak with him, but Joe could not muster much more than a few quiet moans. Hurrying out of the tent, Charley rushed over to Lt. Wallings who had also just come off of picket duty.

"Hurry, sir," he shouted.

"What is it, Charley? I was just off to sleep."

"It's Joe," Charley replied, "he's dying, I'm certain of it. He can barely speak!"

"Then go get the medics," Wallings shot back. "I'll not go in there. Other men are made for things such as this."

Charley gritted his teeth but did as Wallings said and found the medics. He directed them to Joe's tent, and they hurried inside. Moments later, they were carrying him out on a stretcher and loading him into the ambulance cart. As it rode off, Alfred appeared outside his tent.

"Who was that?" he asked.

"It was Joe," Charley replied, his voice raspy from exertion. "He's dreadfully sick, and I'm worried it's the typhoid again."

"Might be," Alfred said, weakly. "It's hard to say. With sickness like this comes things like pneumonia, the flu, and heaven knows what else. He's in the hands of the doctors, now."

"So was Chuck," Charley shot back. "Are we sure they even know what to do? How do we know they can heal him?"

"Can you heal him?" Alfred asked.

"Well, no…"

"So we know that much, at least," Alfred said. "I know I can't, either, and neither can Lt. Wallings or Captain Sweney. I suppose not even Mr. Lincoln can do a thing about it. But maybe the doctors. No one else has a shot, Charley, so give them their chance."

Charley's upper lip curled, but he could not argue. Still, he wanted to know that everything was being done that could be done.

"Will you go?" he asked. "Will you go and check on Joe and see that he's being looked after properly, at least?"

"I'm sick myself, Charley…"

"Tomorrow, then. Please, he's your friend."

"That's not really the issue," Alfred said. "He's ill and so is everyone in the infirmary. If I go there, I put myself at greater risk than staying here in isolation. I am not in so dire a situation as Joe."

"But you're already sick," Charley pleaded.

"It doesn't work like that, Charley. Just because I'm sick doesn't mean I cannot become sicker. We have to trust the doctors to do their best for him. We'll do no good if we expose ourselves to whatever he's attracted."

"But…"

"Charley," Alfred said flatly, "I'm sorry, but this is how it's going to be. Pray for Joe. Other than that, just trust the doctors."

Alfred clearly wanted no further discussion. He returned to his tent and left Charley to stew in his anger alone. Part of him wanted to chase after Alfred, tear down his tent, and curse him for refusing to see to a friend, but he could not bring himself to do such a thing. Instead, he retrieved his drum and strapped it across his shoulder. Walking a short distance from his camp, he began to play.

As he did, his thoughts started to drift as they used to before he came to the war. Back then, he dreamed of marching with the army and leading them into battle. He had seen himself standing boldly as bullets flew past and shells exploded around him. Brave soldiers stood by his side and together they faced down the Rebel armies.

But he had no need to imagine anymore. He had seen it all with his own eyes.

Now, instead, he pictured those streets he had once marched up and down. He saw the boys from his school marching along beside him, blissfully unaware of what really happened when men marched off to war—many did not march back.

Charley wondered if his schoolmates knew that truth. That is, they knew that men died in war, but did they know that people they loved would die? Perhaps some of them had lost fathers and older brothers already. Charley supposed he was lucky he had not lost anyone so close to him, but he had still lost friends. Could any of his classmates say the same? He would not wish that on them, if not.

Charley did not feel regret at his decision to join the army. In fact, he was still proud that he had marched with his fellow Pennsylvanians to defend the nation he loved. His heart had changed, though. The youthful flutter that had danced in his chest when he first marched away was long gone. That first shell at Newport News had dispelled that sort of excitement. It was replaced with a nervous anticipation—one that knew battle was never far off. He did not fear it, but he did not find himself desiring it anymore, either.

It had already become part of life. A simple fact of his every day.

Charley wondered if this was what men like Captain Sweney and Lt. Wallings felt. Perhaps Chuck, when he was still alive, felt this paradoxical ease at the knowledge safety was never fully assured. Was that why a man like General Hancock could sit atop a horse while musket balls flew by, all but daring the Rebels to take his life. Was that bravery? Men like Captain Sweney would say it was. Men like Abel would say it was foolishness.

Charley decided he would rather think like Captain Sweney. With that in mind, Charley resolved to redouble his efforts to conduct all his duties wholeheartedly. He would be a principled man and, thus, he would not flee for anything. That was the promise he made when he joined the army, and that was the promise he made again to himself that day.

★ ★ ★

It was over a week before the sickness began to abate. Alfred was up and about after a few days, though Charley mostly chose to avoid him. He supposed he wasn't terribly angry at him, but he still wished he had been willing to look into Joe's wellbeing. They had not had news of anyone from their company that had been taken to the infirmary. Charley reasoned that was good news, as word of a soldier's death always made its way back to the company, whereas changes in health did not always merit reporting.

For his part, Charley went about his business as he had since the outbreak began. Near the start of August, he was off on the outskirts of camp practicing his drum when he heard an odd sound behind him. It took a moment, but when he recognized it he wheeled around to see Joe headed toward him, fife pressed to his lips. In an instant, Charley dropped his drum to the ground and hurried to meet Joe, who lowered his fife as Charley approached.

"You're alive!" Charley shouted.

"Aye, such as it is," Joe replied. "I feel like I've been dead for days, but they tell me that wasn't the case."

"I was worried," Charley said. "There was no news coming from the infirmary, I suppose because it was so busy, but no one would go check on you. Not even Alfred!"

"Probably the right decision," Joe replied, much to Charley's surprise.

"Really? You don't wish someone had come to see you? He was sick anyway, what could happen?"

"That building, Charley, it's no place for anyone that doesn't absolutely have to be there. If I had known what it would be like when I was being carried away, I might have rolled off and asked to die in camp. I don't think the captain would have liked that much, though."

"I just... you were alone," Charley stammered.

"Well, I had doctors," Joe replied. "And anyway, I was barely aware of what was going on around me. Aside from the sound of men vomiting and the smell of death, there really wasn't much to experience. I'm glad Alfred didn't come. And I'm *very* glad you didn't."

Charley frowned.

"I suppose I shall have to apologize to Alfred."

"I'm sure there's no hard feelings," Joe said. "Anyway, I'm famished. What do we have back at camp?"

"Hard tack and water," Charley replied with a smile. Joe sighed.

"Sounds like just the feast for me."

CHAPTER 16

Coward

August 11, 1862

Once most of the regiment had healed, the order came down to prepare for march. They would be headed back to join the rest of the army and prepared to deploy at a moment's notice. Another piece of news came in, however, of a somewhat more somber tone. President Martin Van Buren, himself a man of the North and an ardent abolitionist later in life, had passed away. The New York regiments took this especially hard, as the man had been governor of their state when many of their parents were younger.

Some of the generals even knew Van Buren personally, and, while he was not so dearly loved during his time as president, his stance against slavery had made him somewhat of a darling among a select few supporters of the Northern cause. For many, however, it was enough to know the Southerners hated the man, whom they saw as one of the greatest disappointments to come out of the Jackson Presidency. He was, as hand-picked successor of Jackson himself, little more than a traitor to them now and evidence that one could never trust a Yankee.

In recognition of Van Buren's achievements, and, with the added pleasure of thumbing their nose at the Southerners, the entire Northern Army held a ceremony in his honor. Colors were presented and a salute was ordered, as many cheered the heroic life of the former president.

For his part, Charley knew barely any facts about the man and he wagered the same was the case with most of the young men assembled.

Charley had been born nine years after Van Buren left office, meaning aside from the officers, only Abel Tyson had even been alive during his presidency. Still, the men showed their reverence for him just the same.

As they did, Charley thought on President Lincoln and how much he had already achieved. Should they win the war, he imagined his exploits would be gilded for eternity and, when the eventuality of his death arrived, he would no doubt receive these honors and far more. It would be a gallant time, for certain, and Charley promised himself that he would travel to wherever festivities were held to celebrate the great man's life.

It did strike him as odd, for a moment, that he was already considering what he would do at the event of the sitting president's death, but Charley supposed that was the way of things when one went to war. You either accept that death can come at any instant or you pretend it can never happen and act without such thoughts weighing on you. It occurred to Charley that either was likely an effective means of keeping one's head in order.

When the ceremony had ended and the men began to fall out, Charley found Alfred and stopped him.

"I wanted to apologize for treating you so harshly over Joe's illness," he said. "You were right, Alfred, and I was wrong."

"I would not say you were wrong," Alfred replied, much to Charley's surprise. "We must remember to care for one another if we are to escape this war with our souls in order. Perhaps I was thinking too hard on my life and forgetting that I am more than a breathing body. Since our conversation I have thought on that quite a bit. So, thank you for that. I am not certain I would have thought it over if not for you."

Charley did not know what to say. It was an odd admission from Alfred that he had in some way been wrong, and stranger still to think a man his age might have learned something from Charley's own anger. He wanted to press him further to better understand his change of heart, but a commotion from just outside the camp demanded both their attention.

Coming up the road from the direction of the western picket line was a small group of guards returning from their duties. In the middle of them all, two men were dragging Abel Tyson. Tyson cursed them, using words fouler than Charley could remember hearing from any grown man outside of an alleyway. When the men arrived in camp, they threw Abel to the ground and one went so far as to spit upon him.

A few moments later, Lt. Wallings appeared and looked quizzically at the scene before him.

"What is all this about?" he asked. "Why is my soldier being so abused?"

"He ain't much of a soldier, I don't think," scoffed one of the picketmen. "We caught this yellow bastard trying to cross the picket line and head north. Lookin' to desert, I'll warrant. Or maybe worse…"

"Damn you," Abel growled, "I told you what I was up to. I heard there was pheasant up that-a-ways and I went lookin' for a bit extra before we marched."

Abel, rising to his knees, turned to Lt. Wallings and began to plead with him.

"It's the truth, sir," he said. "I just wanted to nab me a bird. We've had naught but hard tack, water, and the occasional blood sausage. I've caught a rabbit or two since we've been here, but the damn things is so scrawny they don't amount to nothin'. You've gotta believe me, lieutenant."

Wallings looked down at him with a frown.

"Are yeh sure about that story, Tyson?" he replied, his skepticism palpable. "Are yeh sure yeh didn't maybe see an opportunity to run while the rest of the brigade was occupied with the ceremony? Because that seems like just the kind of thing a little yellow bastard like you might do, run away while we honor a true hero."

"No, lieutenant, no!" Abel cried. "I didn't! I wasn't running!"

Wallings considered his pleas for a moment and then looked over at Charley and Alfred.

"What do you boys think?" he asked. "You know him just as well as anyone. Do you think he was out hunting pheasants?"

"My ass," Alfred replied without a moment's hesitation. "He's been planning to run since he was mustered in. Any one of us can attest to it. The man's as yellow as they come."

"You rotten little bugger!" Abel yelled, and lurched to his feet, trying to run at Alfred. Before he made it half a step, one of the guards had clobbered him with his rifle. Abel fell to the dirt and let out a long, wavering cry. Wallings looked down at him with disgust.

"Get this vermin out of my sight," he said. "To the brig with him, and captain will decide how to deal with him in the morning."

The guards agreed, dragging Abel away, as he continued his pitiful cries. Charley watched as he was thrown into the brig, and could not help but shake his head.

"I didn't think he'd actually do it," he said. "Did you ever think he would?"

"I had a feeling," Alfred replied. "The man was without principle. He had no reason to be here. Once he saw what he was really facing, then got a taste of the calm after, he wasn't ready to move again. I'll wager news that we were headed out got to him and he bolted. Makes sense, but doesn't make him any less of a coward."

"What's gonna happen to him?" Charley asked.

"I wager you'll see," Alfred answered. "Soon enough, I'll wager…"

★ ★ ★

Charley needed only to wait until the following morning to see how the army treated deserters. Captain Sweney had the men form up and brought Charley out front to play the cadence for execution. While the captain had already told Charley that they would not go so far as to kill Abel, the sound still brought a chill to the otherwise searing heat of the morning. The entire regiment stood by, watching as the ceremony commenced.

As Charley played the march to execution, Tyson was dragged out in chains. His captors tossed him into the mud, where he lay for several moments, writhing in anguish. He called out to the others to let him go, but not a man even considered breaking ranks. They all waited patiently until Captain Sweney stepped forward.

"Abel Tyson," Sweney roared, "you are guilty of cowardice and absenting yourself without leave from the regiment while in the face of the enemy. By order of the Commander in Chief of the United States Military, President Abraham Lincoln, you are hereby sentenced. You will forfeit ten dollars out of your wages and be confined for no less than two years in military prison assigned to hard labor. And you're damned lucky we don't execute you."

The men cheered at this, which surprised Charley. He reasoned, however, that the men were rife with stress at the order to march. It was no different than the reasoning Alfred had given for Abel's desertion, but warranted as these men were not cowards. To see one of their own so brazenly shirk his duty no doubt raised great ire in them.

Charley soon realized the extent of that ire extended far beyond what he himself felt. As soon as the captain turned his back, Lt. Wallings grabbed Abel by the shoulder and leaned in close to his ear.

"You didn't think that was all you'd be getting, did ya?"

A moment later, the rest of the company was on him. They pulled back his hair and shaved half of it off with a dull razor. Abel cried out the entire time, and Charley could not help but feel pity for the man. It was horribly shocking, but the rest of the company showed no signs of mercy.

Once he was shaven, they forced him to his feet and placed a board upon his back that read, "coward." Then, Wallings turned to Charley and said,

"'The Rogue's March,' Charley. Mr. Tyson is going on parade."

Charley complied, though it made him quite ill to do so. At least he was spared looking at Abel as he led on. Wallings marched beside him as he led Abel through the camp, playing "The Rogue's March" all the while. They snaked through the camp, making sure to pass every regiment in the brigade so that all the soldiers there assembled might see what reward a coward receives in the Union Army.

When, at long last, the march was over, Abel was led back to the brig and tossed inside with his sign still strapped to his back. The rest of the company dispersed, leaving Charley alone with his thoughts. He thought it strange that he should pity Abel, but the man did make quite a pathetic scene. It was hard not to have some feeling for the man who had marched beside him since muster.

As he stood alone, Charley was approached by Captain Sweney, who seemed to have a rare moment of respite.

"Thinking hard, Charley?" he asked.

"I suppose," Charley replied.

"And what on?"

"Well... I suppose on the morning. I wonder, have you ever thought about running from battle, Captain?"

Capt. Sweney looked down at Charley, staring deep into his eyes as if trying to determine some hidden meaning in his question.

"Have *you* felt the urge to run?" he asked.

"Not at all," Charley replied, having no reason to lie. Capt. Sweney frowned, perhaps realizing that there was nothing behind the question but curiosity. He took a few moments to consider the question before answering.

"It would not matter if I did."

Charley's brow furrowed. He hadn't expected such a response.

"What I mean to say is," Capt. Sweney continued, "any fear I feel is meaningless. My position requires me to both take and give orders. I make no major decisions on my own, but I must watch as the consequences of my orders unfold, so what right have I to think of running? Furthermore, I believe in the men who give me my orders. They are far wiser than I am, and thus I will do as they order to the best of my ability."

"But don't you ever question the orders they give?" Charley asked. "In the trench, back at the marsh... it seemed like..."

"It would be best if we did not speak of that further," Sweney said. "I was not at my best. Even if I do question the orders I am given, I should never let you and the rest of the boys know that. It is difficult to order men into a situation you know will threaten their lives, but it is even more difficult to trust that the orders you are given are wise. The men of this company grant me that trust. In exchange, I owe them both my most wise discretion and my absolute trust in the wisdom of our leaders. No one of us can see the entirety of the grand strategy laid out by our generals. We can only execute our orders to the best of our ability."

Charley tried to imagine what it must feel like to have to both trust and ask for trust, but it was beyond him. He believed in Captain Sweney, and he believed in Col. Irwin and Gen. Hancock because of that. That, he supposed, would have to be enough. As he thought about it, though, he was stricken with thoughts of his company men who had fallen.

"How do you do it, then?" he asked. "How do you see your men die? If you are only in the middle of a chain of orders, isn't it hard to see men die as a result of events beyond your control?"

"It's impossible," Captain Sweney replied, "but that also is one of the few thoughts that allows me to continue. Out on the battlefield, any man can be killed at any moment, be they private, captain, colonel, or general. Men like General Hancock take the field anyway. The same is true for Colonel Irwin; the same has to be true for me. That, I suppose is the comfort. I ask you men to risk death, and I must ensure that I risk it myself. Any of us may die at any moment, myself included."

"And the drummer boy?" Charley asked.

"Not if I have any say in it, Charley," Captain Sweney replied, with a cold defiance. It was hollow, though. Charley knew this to be true from the captain's own words.

"Do you?" he asked, not meaning to be so pointed. But he could not help it. Something compelled him to ask, but nothing could compel Captain Sweney to answer. Instead, his face fell and he simply turned away, walking off in search of his next set of orders.

CHAPTER 17

Long Withdrawal

The men of the 49th quickly put the spectacle of Abel's punishment behind them as the army continued to withdraw toward the north. Covering the maneuver involved an odd sort of practice, which, while Charley understood the tactic behind it, seemed nearly too comical to believe. Being situated at the rear of the brigade, the 49th was tasked with guarding the rear and creating any sort of diversion they could to cover the withdrawal. It was the diversion that Charley and many others in the company could not help but be amused by.

They laughed, at first, when Captain Sweney gave the order to start stuffing spare uniforms with brush and hay, but his stern look told them this was no joke. They did so hurriedly, creating several dozen dummy soldiers, each with what appeared at a distance to be a gun in their hand. When this was finished, the dummies were placed one every fifty yards or so to give the appearance of a picket line. Charley found it hard to believe this tactic would trick anyone, but Lt. Wallings assured him that from far off they looked no different than real soldiers and, unless the Rebels were planning to attack the line, they would likely not catch on to the ruse for at least several hours.

Charley trusted that the officers were correct and helped to erect the last of the picket dummies. Then, at about 5 pm, the 49th finally moved out, bidding farewell to Harrison's Landing and heading east toward Charles City and, beyond it, Yorktown. The march lasted over five hours, taking them four miles past the city and at least two miles past where Charley felt he could not march any farther. Still, they continued on until they had nearly arrived at the spot they planned to make camp.

Just at the outskirts of that location, there was a small stream which needed to be crossed. Whether it was the long wearying day or simply a case of mass confusion, the officers could not agree on the best manner in which to cross the creek. For several minutes, they discussed their options while the foot-weary soldiers waited, some more patiently than others. Finally, after what seemed like an eternity, a voice called out from behind Company D.

"Men, step in the water! You will camp soon."

Already irritated by the delay, Sergeant Cunningham of Company D shot back, "Damn you, get in yourself!"

As the men looked about to see who had called to them, a low murmur began to circulate. Slowly, they stepped aside as the man in question made his way through the crowd and down to the stream. He took one look at Sgt. Cunningham, who immediately snapped into a sheepish salute. The officer, dressed in the regalia of a major general, stepped into the water without further delay and trudged off toward the camp, soaking his trousers up to the knee as he went.

Once he had crossed, he looked back at the sergeant, who now quietly backed away, attempting to disappear into the ranks of his company. Shaking his head, the general continued off to the camp.

When he was out of earshot, the others in Company F began to whisper, wondering who the general had been. All but Charley and Alfred, who had seen the man days before as he accepted their captured munitions.

Soon, the rest of the company caught on that the man had been none other than Major General McClellan and they could not help but roar with laughter. Charley, too, had to chuckle. The moment of good humor was a welcome change from the struggles of the past several weeks. He was downright cheerful when the regiment made their way into camp and set up their tents, and within minutes of lying down he was fast asleep.

Over the next few days, the army made its way down the Virginia Peninsula, retracing the steps they had fought so hard to cover when they had first arrived. When the city came into view, Charley thought on their last stay. His mind wandered to Lenny's death, and he wondered if they might pass by his burial place. During a short break in the march, Charley sought out Alfred.

"Do you remember, is Lenny buried nearby here?" he asked, when he had found him. Alfred frowned and looked around, racking his brain to remember.

"You know, I think he is," Alfred replied. "If I remember, the picket line was just up to the north some few hundred yards. He'd be, perhaps, two hundred yards east of this point if we were to walk straight north from here."

"Do you think Captain Sweney might let us visit the spot?" Charley asked.

"I will ask him," Alfred replied. "As we speak of it, I feel a deep regret that we did not bring you to give your last respects when he first passed. It falls to me to remedy that."

Alfred hurried over to find Captain Sweney and gave him a smart salute. Charley watched as they spoke, each casting a glance over toward him as they exchanged words. After a few moments, Alfred returned with a smile on his face.

"If we move quickly we can go to the grave," Alfred said. "We'll be on the march again soon, though, so we need to meet the company as they pass. So we'd better get moving."

"May I come with you?" Joe piped in.

"Come on, then," Alfred replied, and the three trotted off toward the old picket line. The remnants of the line still stood, with the exception of a few areas that had been cleared to allow wider columns of troops to move through. They followed along the line for a few hundred yards before Alfred stopped and peered out at the field around them.

"There it is," he muttered, and struck out toward a small wooden cross that rose out of the ground. When they arrived, Charley could barely make out a slight rise in the dirt on which grass had already begun to grow. Ragweed lined the area around the wooden memorial and looked almost as though someone had planted flowers on the grave. Alfred noticed Charley eying the weed and shrugged.

"It was the best we could find at the time," he said. "I would have liked something better, but Chuck said a soldier's grave ought to be bare, at least until the war is won. I'm not sure what he meant by that. Suppose I won't get to ask."

As he spoke, Charley knelt down by the side of the grave and placed a hand on the dirt.

"We miss you, Lenny," he said. "Alfred had your banjo sent home, so your mama has it now. The music hasn't been the same since you died. I'm sorry to say it, but not one of us knows half as many songs as you, and there ain't a voice among us that sings half as well, either. I hope you're resting well."

They stood there in silence for several minutes, none knowing what more there could be to say. Finally, Charley rose to his feet and slung his drum around to the front. Without pause, Joe drew out his fife and raised it to his mouth. Charley beat out the opening roll to "The Minstrel Boy," and Joe followed along, playing the tune loud and slow. Alfred mouthed the words in silence as they played through.

When they were finished, all three lowered their heads and Charley did his best to fight back tears, but he could not manage. The droplets fell, splashing on his drum. After a moment, he raised his chin in defiance and began to beat out another tune. Joe looked at him and nodded, his own face becoming hard with determination. All three came to attention and turned toward the path where their fellow soldiers were marching along.

Side by side, Charley, Joe, and Alfred struck out toward the line, playing "The Battle Hymn of the Republic." As they neared the line, another group of fifes and drums took up the song. The three stopped beside the column and continued to play. Each regiment that passed picked up the tune, joining them as they marched through. They had played it ten times through before the 49th Pennsylvania reached them and they fell in, continuing the tune as they struck onward.

★ ★ ★

The tail end of the army's long withdrawal saw the 49th climbing aboard a steamer called *Montreal* on Friday, August 22. It took only a day for the steamer to carry them up the Potomac and drop them back outside Alexandria once again. It was an odd feeling being suddenly so far away from the war. In the city nearby, men and women were going about their business much as they had before fighting started. Children Charley's age were filing into schoolhouses or preparing for the harvest with their families.

Back home, his father was no doubt hard at work mending clothes and making suits. Perhaps he was even sewing uniforms for the next batch of Union recruits. His brother Lewis would be eleven by now, and likely scurrying about the shop when he was not in school. Soon enough he would join their father in the business, Charley was certain. He was already replacing buttons and mending toys for the neighborhood children. Some days there would be a line of girls waiting for him to sew up their doll's clothing. Lewis would be just fine, Charley knew. He was going to be an excellent tailor.

For his part, Charley did not know what he would do after the war. It seemed silly to think about it at this point. Maybe he would become a tailor as well. Maybe he would remain in the army and become an officer like Captain Sweney. Perhaps he would even become a general one day, but that was far off. The only thing he could do now was focus on the day in front of him.

That particular day, there were several different regiments moving through the area. Some were headed to defensive positions, others were joining already established corps. One in particular quickly became of interest to the 49th the moment they were spotted. Alfred recognized their insignia first, but when they raised their state flag everyone could see they were boys from their own home.

Being without orders for the moment, many of the men from each regiment came together to greet one another. The 125th Pennsylvania Volunteers, as they turned out to be, had been mustered in following Governor Curtin's call for 21 new regiments. They were quite fresh, having been formed earlier in the month, and their uniforms were well pressed and spotless. Alfred shook his head, looking the men up and down.

"Tell me I looked like that once," he said.

"Like what?" a man of the 125th replied with a laugh.

"So damned clean," Alfred said. "I swear my uniform was never so blue as the one you're wearing."

"You look like you've been camping in a sty for ten years," the man replied. "I can't seem to fathom how a man could take such a beating in a few short months."

"You'll figure out how soon enough, I imagine," Alfred said. "Anyway, Alfred Moulder's the name. Myself and much of the regiment are out of Chester County. West Chester to be specific for myself and young Charley, here."

The man looked down at Charley with momentary surprise that quickly changed to understanding.

"Ah, the little drummer boy," he said. "I've read about you in the paper. You do not look quite so little anymore. War has made a man of you. The name is Michael O'Donnell, by the way. Good to meet the both of you."

"Likewise," Alfred replied. "Any idea what corps you boys are being attached to? I think we'd be glad of a few more Pennsylvania men to hold the line beside us. You'll need a little breaking in, though…"

"My understanding is we're soon to get it," Michael said. "Word has trickled up that General Lee is planning to invade the North. I'm not certain how he intends to do that, but if he gives it a try we'll spank him and his Rebel boys like a lot of school children."

"That's the spirit," Alfred Chucked, "but don't sleep on these southerners, friend. The last few months have not been a long string of victories. It's been hard-fought and there's not been a lot to show for it. Richmond still stands and much of our gains in Virginia are forfeited. I reckon that's what gives old General Lee the confidence to come north."

"I suppose so," Michael replied, his mood somewhat dampened.

"No need to fret, though," Alfred said, clapping the man on his shoulder. "Tough or not, they ain't bulletproof, and us Northern boys are pretty tough ourselves, especially the men of Pennsylvania."

"Keystone of the Union still, ain't it?" Michael said with a smile.

"Sure as you're born, friend," Alfred replied. With that, orders came in for the two regiments to form back up and the boys said their goodbyes. And as the closing days of August began to fade, the Army of the South was on the move…

CHAPTER 18

Crampton's Gap

The days that followed were a confusing jumble of marching orders, relocations, making camp, and running drills. By the time September came, Charley could barely remember where they had been in the week prior, or what the thought behind their constant movement might have been. That became clear, however, soon after the turn of the month.

By the first week of September, General Lee's invasion of the North was a known fact. His plan, it seemed, was to use the momentum he had gained after taking over the Southern army during the Peninsula Campaign to move quickly into Maryland and smash the Union forces still working to regroup. General McClellan was determined to allow no such thing and sent his battle-hardened men to meet them along with several fresh regiments from Pennsylvania and several other Northern states.

The 49th, of course, was part of the push to cut off Lee before he could make any significant headway into Maryland. They moved quickly from the D.C. area to Tennellytown, and then to Rockville, onto Dawson, to Bannerville, and finally to Sugarloaf Mountain where, on September 11, part of the corps was engaged in battle with the Rebels. Charley could hear the battle in the far-off distance as the 49th awaited orders, but none came. Instead, Colonel Irwin spent the day pacing up and down the line, making sure the regiment was prepared should anything happen.

On that particular day, they were spared the battle, but they could hear skirmishes continuing in the distance. The following day news came in that the Confederates had moved on Harper's Ferry, some 25 miles away from their position at Sugarloaf Mountain. The battle there was hot, and the Union boys were giving as good as they got.

"There may soon be a decisive battle," Irwin allowed, "but you can be sure that it won't happen without the 49th. Ain't a thing decided until the boys of Pennsylvania have their say!"

The men cheered at this and Charley joined his voice with the others. Irwin's rally call lifted their spirits enough to keep them marching,

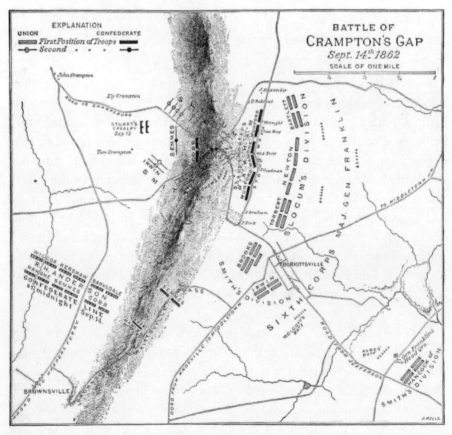

One day before the battle of Crampton's Gap, General George McClellan had received a copy of Gen. Lee's battle plan, including the revelation that Lee's army was divided in an attempt to capture Harper's Ferry. Confederate artillery was placed on the north hill of Crampton's Gap and three infantry regiments were placed there to guard them. McClellan ordered Maj. Gen. William Franklin's Sixth Corps (of which the 49th PA was a part) to take the gap and push the artillery off the heights. (Buel and Johnson, *Battles and Leaders of the Civil War* (New York: The Century Co., 1887)

but it was the news that came the following day that really picked up the men.

Early in the morning on September 14, word came down that the Rebels had held up nearby in a place called Crampton's Gap. General Lee had split his men, it seemed, in an attempt to slow the Union army until after they had achieved their goals in the area. Their corps was to make sure this maneuver failed. As they marched, Charley could see the men itching for a fight. Even Alfred seemed intently focused on the battle before them.

It was not long before they were in sight of the enemy. Col. Irwin led the 49th out to the left flank of the battle just southwest of Burkittsville, where they could see the Rebel army in position all the way up to the summit. As the 49th reached their position, the Confederate artillery opened fire on them from their vantage halfway up the nearby mountains.

Poised and ready to do battle, the corps paused.

Artillery shells continued to explode around them as the long line of the corps stretched out along the mountain range. They outnumbered the enemy substantially and, despite the Rebels' advantage of position, there was no reason to believe they could withstand an attack by a superior force.

Yet, the corps paused.

When they had been standing in ranks for nearly two hours, Captain Sweney finally broke and rode off to where Colonel Irwin stood surveying the field in front of them.

"What the hell are we doing, Colonel?" he cried. "We're nothing but target practice for those Rebel guns. Why haven't we moved?"

"Your guess is as good as mine, Captain," Irwin replied. "Perhaps our artillery support is not yet ready. Though, they have held their current position since noon and it must be near to two. I cannot say."

Unsatisfied, but unwilling to further question orders, Capt. Sweney rode back to the line and fell in amongst his company.

"Any word on when the attack will come?" Joe asked, shifting back and forth to spare his stiffening legs.

"Sometime in September is the best I can tell you," Sweney grumbled. "Perhaps October if the general is so inclined."

The words were followed by grumbling from amongst the men, but happily, they were not to come true. Instead, the army began to move forward an hour later, at 3 pm. A barrage of artillery fire supported their advance and they lurched toward the enemy line to the sound of Charley's beating drum.

The world again turned to smoke and fire as ordnance rained down upon them, the buzzing bullets finding their marks as the soldiers plunged forward. Charley's eyes darted all around, noticing the growing number of men falling out of the ranks and flat onto the ground. He had been on the other side of the field before with the enemy approaching, but this was his first experience as part of an assault.

The two positions could not be more different.

When holding the line, the men could crouch and watch as the enemy approached. They were offered some protection from a ditch, fence, or stone wall and used it the best they could. Defenders could fire at will, drop to reload, and pick out their target before firing. Sitting still was not so fatiguing and, should a defending soldier grow weary, they could duck for a few moments to steady themselves. An advancing army had none of those advantages.

There was no protection for them. Standing shoulder to shoulder, they plunged forward even as shells exploded around them. Even at the back corner of the company, Charley felt a harrowing fear grip him. Still, he moved forward.

The others, he was certain, felt that fear as well. Still they moved forward.

Once they were close to the Confederate line, they paused and lowered their weapons, taking up positions in staggered lines.

First line. Fire! Kneel.

Second line. Fire! Kneel.

Third line. Fire! Kneel.

And then they were on the move again, striding boldly toward the enemy position. They repeated the exercise again and again, inching forward while cannon and musket ball crashed into their ranks. Charley watched as one man, a private from Company C, took aim, fired, and then knelt to reload. As he did, a bullet caught him in the shoulder.

He stumbled back and tried to steady himself, but when he managed to stand again another bullet found him, shattering the bone above his eye and snuffing out his life in an instant.

On the other side of him, a cannon ball tore through Company G and sent men hurtling through the sky. One man landed on another soldier, who tumbled over onto the ground and did not stand up again. Charley had no time to consider what had happened, as the line continued forward and he thundered out the advance. The rapping of his drum was barely audible over the chorus of muskets and cannon, but he struck it just the same. Beside him, Joe played on, though Charley could see the fear in his eyes.

Then, like the sudden clearing of a terrible thunderstorm, the Rebel line broke. They fled back from their trenches and into the mountains where their reserves had set up a vantage point near the summit next to Crampton's Gap. The Sixth Corps hurried them on their way with a continuous volley of musket fire until they were hunkered down at their new position. A rally cry rose from up above along the mountains and the Rebels prepared for a new defensive.

"Can you believe they haven't had enough?" Captain Sweney cried.

"Aye," Lt. Wallings called back, "because I ain't had enough of whoopin' 'em!"

A great roar rolled over the 49th at the old lieutenant's pronouncement and, a moment later, the order was received to pursue the enemy and push them off of the Gap for good. The boys were riding high and gladly pushed forward, ready to make the enemy regret their decision to rally. The First New Jersey Brigade led the way as the barrage from the Rebel line continued. It was far weaker than it had been before they took to the hills. They put up a half-hearted defense as the energized Union soldiers continued their spirited charge.

Finally, the advance proved too much for the Southerners and they fled. Within 15 minutes of reengaging the enemy, they had been sent scattering in all directions. The battle over, the officers paused to take stock of the situation. As they did, the enlisted men were put at ease, but ordered to stay close to their company. The next order to move might come at any moment.

As they waited in the slowly clearing fog of battle, Charley looked over the field behind him and saw it littered with blue-clad men. They had paid dearly for the victory at Crampton's Gap, and the 49th Pennsylvania was in no way spared. Alfred estimated the corps lost near a thousand men all told, but he could not be sure. That would make it the bloodiest day the 49th had yet faced. The numbers didn't interest Charley, so much as the fact that Company F was largely not affected. He was happy not to have lost any more friends.

"How long do you think it'll be before move again?" Charley asked Alfred, who was standing nearby.

"Not long," Alfred said, taking a knee. "Last I heard the whole of Lee's army is moving in this area. I'll wager the whole of the Army of the Potomac is around here, too. If Lee truly wants to invade the North, he's going to have to try the whole damn army. The board's nearly set, Charley, and we're a piece soon to be moved."

"Any guess where we're moving to?" Charley asked. Alfred just shrugged, but as he did, Captain Sweney stepped in between them.

"Orders are in," he said. "We're headed toward Sharpsburg, Maryland, to take up position near a little creek called the Antietam."

CHAPTER 19

Sharpsburg

The 49th Pennsylvania, along with the rest of the Sixth Corps, moved early in the morning of September 16. They left Crampton's Gap headed north past Rohrersville before the sun had risen, moving quickly as they could toward the town of Sharpsburg. There was an odd quiet in the air that hung about them as they marched. Something electric that none of them could quite grasp, but all of them could feel.

Messengers came and went as they traveled along, reporting troop movements and minor skirmishes to Col. Irwin, which he relayed to the captains. The rest of the men picked up what information they could from comments overheard and passed back along the line. General Lee's men were on the move toward Sharpsburg, or else, they had already arrived. Shots were being fired near the creek or perhaps a few regiments had recently taken up position near the creek. The exact truth was hard to discern, but the Sixth Corps' destination remained the same—they were headed for the northeast corner of the town, ready to stop the Rebels from moving closer to the 49th's beloved Pennsylvania.

They marched through the entire day and made camp late in the evening. Musket fire could be heard nearby, but they were ordered to hold their ground. Word filtered down that General Hooker had crossed the creek and was advancing to take a position north of the town, meeting Rebel resistance as he went. Artillery thundered in the distance as well, firing from both sides of the line. The noise was so loud that Charley thought there must have been near a dozen batteries all firing at once.

The northern end of the field where the battle of Antietam was fought. This map shows the areas where the earliest action occurred: the East Woods, Cornfield, Dunker Church, and West Woods. The 49th Pennsylvania Infantry arrived after an overnight forced march to reinforce the area. (Antietam Battlefield Board, "Battle of Antietam, 7:20 AM," *Antietam Battlefield Atlas*, 1904)

Captain Sweney stood a few feet away, and Charley leaned over and whispered to him.

"It sounds like the whole of both armies is here today," he said.

"That may be the case," Sweney replied. "Lee has made quite a push, so I have heard. McClellan has brought all his forces to counter the advance. There must be nigh on a hundred-thousand men converging on Sharpsburg as we speak. Some more optimistic men are saying the war may be over when this is all said and done."

"What do you say?" Charley asked.

Captain Sweney shrugged.

"The war is over when Mr. Lincoln sends me home."

"Or a Rebel musket does," John put in with a bitter hiss. Charley shot him a quizzical look, but the private quickly turned away.

"Belay that nonsense," Sweney hissed. "You sound like that bloody fool Tyson. We don't need any more of that. If you speak again it had damn well better be to recite 'The Battle Hymn of the Republic.'"

"I suppose he is right, though," Alfred offered. "Those are our two options."

"Not you, too, Moulder," Sweney replied. "When did you become a fatalist?"

"Not at all, sir," Alfred said, "I apologize. I suppose it's just the scale of it all, sir. A hundred-thousand men all converging on one little plot of land. There won't be a clear acre to be seen. Hard for the enemy to miss when there's nothin' but soldiers as far as you can see."

Lt. Wallings appeared from the line to offer his thoughts as well.

"Then it ought to be easy to take a few of those traitors with you before you go, eh?" he said.

"I suppose it ought," Alfred replied.

There was little more to say as the evening wore on. Not a man could catch more than a few minutes of sleep as the sharp anticipation of battle hung over them. The constant echo of artillery fire was no help either. There was no respite from the sounds of skirmishing and, by the time dawn's fingers began to snake across the sky, drums could be heard thumping out the advance across the creek.

At 6 am, they received the order to march. The 49th formed up as they had done so many times before and followed the rest of the corps toward the battle, the sound of which was rolling over the corn fields and filling the sky. Charley thought he could even smell the wafting smoke as they marched toward Antietam Creek. The heavy fog around them made it seem as though they were already in the midst of battle.

However, it was not until they took position atop a high hill midway between Sharpsburg and Keedeysville that they were able to see the fighting they'd heard earlier. They held position there, watching as their fellow Union boys advanced out of the woods north of the city. Directly to their south stood a wide cornfield and from their vantage point they could see the Rebel soldiers lying in wait.

As they watched, Lt. Wallings leaned in toward Captain Sweney and said,

"Old General Hooker can see those Rebel boys in the field, don't you think?"

"He ain't acting like he can," Sweney replied.

"Wait now, he's stopping," Alfred called out. "Looks like he's spotted 'em."

The men of the 49th could only watch as General Hooker's corps stopped and held position just outside the cornfield. A few moments later, they saw the Union artillery begin to change their trajectory, targeting the cornfield with every gun available. Suddenly, the air was hot with shell and canister as the Union batteries rained fire upon the Confederates in the cornfield. Charley looked down at the melee below to see men thrown into the air, tossed aside, and torn apart by the volley.

While the artillery continued to unleash torrents of lead upon the enemy, the Union soldiers began to fix bayonets. The Rebels in the cornfield were under heavy fire, but they refused to withdraw. Or, perhaps the order to withdraw had been given but none could hear over the crash of Union ordinance. Whatever the case, they held their ground as the barrage ended and the infantry renewed their advance.

There was no time for the smoke to clear before the two forces met amongst the head-high stalks of corn. From their vantage on the hill, the 49th could see the two sides clash, hacking mercilessly at one another with bayonets and clubbing each other with rifle butts. Men screamed in agony as bullets and bayonets tore through flesh, and within minutes the field was covered in bodies of blue and gray alike.

Slowly, the Union force began to push the Rebels back and out of the cornfield, but it was short lived. The Confederates pushed back, bringing up more soldiers to contest the area and pile more dead upon the ground. There was no way to tell who truly had the upper hand, as both sides inflicted heavy slaughter upon the other, losing ground and regaining it, only to lose it once more.

"Now I have seen hell," Alfred whispered, and the others could not help but agree.

Below, the battle continued. The rest of the battle was difficult to see from their vantage point. A large Union force was making headway further west, but without sufficient success to come to the aid of their men in the cornfield. After just over an hour of fighting, another detachment of Confederates arrived and began to push back against the Northerners. As the tide turned once more, the men began to look about for the officers and wonder what they were doing holding back when the field in front of them was so hotly contested.

For their part, the officers remained calm and poised for action, whenever they might be called upon. As the morning wore on, however, no call came. Down below, the battle became a clear stalemate, with Hooker finally pushing the Rebels out of the cornfield and the Rebels falling back to hold the line closer to Sharpsburg. They took up positions across the field from one another and hunkered down.

As late morning approached, the sounds of battle could be heard to the south. General Hancock rode past to make certain the men were ready. Stopping before the 49th, he called out to them,

"Boys, do as you have done before; be brave and true, and I think this will be your last battle."

Without another word, he rode off, leaving the men to wonder what sort of premonition the general had received. A few minutes later, they received the order to march south and followed it with great zeal. While the massacre before them had stricken their hearts with no little amount of fear, they also felt anger at the violence inflicted on their fellow Northerners. The 49th, and surely the entire Sixth Corps, was ready to pay the Rebels back in kind.

They had only traveled a short way, however, before a messenger from General McClellan rode up and came to a stop in front of General Hancock.

"Where are you taking these men?" the messenger asked.

"I thought I might take them to war," Hancock shot back, "they look like soldiers to me."

"No, sir," the messenger replied, "your orders are to remain in the North and reinforce General Hooker."

"Tell General McClellan that the action has all but passed here. If my men are to help decide this battle, they must join the fray."

"You can tell the general yourself," the messenger said, "once you have taken up position with General Hooker's troops. If you have a word with him before that, it would not surprise me if he were to strip you of your command."

General Hancock grew hot, but he said no more. Wheeling about, he ordered the men to change direction and head northwest. Many a man voiced their displeasure at the order, but Hancock waved them off. Amongst Company F, there were many a disaffected man.

"The battle is to the south," Alfred grumbled. "Are we to stay here and *watch* it without having any say in its outcome?"

"If that's the general's orders," Captain Sweney replied, though clearly not pleased.

"You know me," Lt. Wallings put in, "I'm not one to complain, but watching our boys get smacked about by those Rebels put a fire in my blood. I'll be damned if I'm going to leave the field without giving them a little back."

"Orders are orders," Captain Sweney said. "I have a feeling we've yet got a part to play in this war, though. Pennsylvania will have its say."

The 49th Pennsylvania moved in double-quick. Word circulated that there was a group of Rebels trying to take up an advantageous position nearby and they were to discourage them from doing so. They made lines and hurried toward their new position. When they arrived, Colonel Irwin called out,

"Steady, right dress!" and the men held.

Behind them, a Union battery was moving full gallop and they slid right a bit to make an opening for them. The position was taken just in time, as the Rebels had arrived near their desired point when the batteries opened fire on them, pushing them back before they could dig in. The men of the 49th cheered as the Rebels pulled back and then took up the line as best they could. They were joined in their position by the 6th Maine Regiment, who lined up to their left.

Colonel Irwin ordered Company C to move forward and act as skirmishers, should the Rebels try to retake the position. Charley could hear an exchange of fire immediately to their left, but he could not see any movement from the Rebels nearby. It was clear, however, that the fighting was very severe, and the world was alive with fire. A flurry of activity occurred in little more than five minutes time, as the remains of General Richardson's division limped into the line to join General Hancock's men. Shortly after, Hancock sent down a messenger to Colonel Irwin.

"Sir," the messenger said, "orders from General Hancock are for you to take command of a brigade of Richardson's division. Hancock himself has been placed in command of the Second Corps!"

Col. Irwin looked at the man with furrowed brow.

"A damned brigade? I've got men here awaiting further orders."

"That's what the general said, Colonel," the messenger told him, and rode off without further words. Col. Irwin turned to the men and shook his head.

"Alright then," he called, shouting over the din of battle. "Major Hulings, to me!"

Maj. Hulings appeared a moment later, looking just as quizzical as the colonel had moments before.

"Sir?"

"The regiment is yours, Major," Irwin said. "Keep them steady and change out those skirmishers before nightfall."

"Aye, sir" Hulings replied. With that, Col. Irwin rode off to his new assignment. As he did, he passed a line of soldiers filing out of the cornfield. The men were bloodied, many limping and some nearly being dragged away. Charley knew them in an instant.

"The 125th," he said. Alfred turned to him and then looked up at the men passing by.

"Lord Almighty," he whispered. Then, waving his hand, he called out to them.

"Huzzah, men of Pennsylvania!" he cried. "Well fought."

A few of the men looked up through glassy eyes, and one or two nodded their appreciation. For the most part, however, they simply continued to make their way to the back of the lines, unhearing or uninterested in his greeting.

"Is Private O'Donnell among you?" he said, in spite of the regiment's seeming disinterest in him. One or two looked up but said nothing.

"Private Michael O'Donnell," he clarified. One man stopped and looked Alfred dead in the eye.

"He's back there," he replied, gesturing toward the cornfield, "if you want to find him. Doubt you'll like what you see though."

Alfred's face fell, as the rest of the 125th continued on their way. He shook his head, turning back to look out at the field before them.

"That's a damned shame," he said. "Curse these traitors. If today is to be the last battle of the war I say we draw it out long as we can. Show these Rebels what happens when you betray your nation."

"Settle down, Private," Captain Sweney said. "Stand tight and stay alert. Don't go dreaming of battle so deeply you miss it when it comes."

"Yes, sir," Alfred replied.

Shortly after Irwin had left to assume his new command, General Hancock came riding up to the line. Major Hulings stepped forward as he approached.

"Something wrong, sir?" Hulings asked, as Hancock looked them over.

"I've surveyed the area," he answered, "and there's a Rebel battery being run out this way. Have your men move back 20 paces. That ought to put you out of range."

Hulings wheeled about and relayed the order, just in the nick of time. As the 49th began to fall back, they heard a loud artillery barrage launch from not far ahead. Hurrying backward, they were nearly out of reach by the time the shells began to land. Charley was near the rear of the company as they withdrew and turned back just for a moment to see the incoming ordinance. The whistling sound of cannon shells grew nearly deafening, and he turned to sprint after the others... but it was too late.

CHAPTER 20

His Last Full Measure

Charley was not sure what had happened at first. He heard the crashing of cannon shells and felt a sharp sting in his abdomen, sending him stumbling toward the others. A moment later, he was teetering over, and the ground came rushing toward him. He was caught, though, and spared the fall. He turned to see the face of an unfamiliar man of the 6th Maine Regiment.

"Are you alright, son?" the man asked. "Were you hit?"

Charley nodded, glancing down at the spot where the shrapnel had pierced him. Blood was beginning to leak out as the man lowered him to the ground.

"I'm Charley," he said, his voice barely raising above a whisper.

"I know who you are, Charley," he replied. "Most of the brigade knows who you are. My name is Bowles. H. H. Bowles, of Maine."

"Maine," Charley nodded. "Hot down here, isn't it?"

Bowles nodded.

"That it is."

A moment later, Captain Sweney appeared by his side and with him Joe and Alfred. Captain Sweney checked the wound on Charley's torso, and then turned him a bit to see the other side.

"It's gone all the way through the body," he said.

"Is that good or bad?" Joe asked.

"There is no good in this situation," Alfred replied.

"We've got to get him back to the medical tents," Sweney ordered. "You three need to carry him back, alright? Right away."

"Er, sir, the battle…" Bowles started, but Sweney cut him off.

"There's no damned battle here," he roared. "Get the boy back and then you can rejoin your unit. But get on with it."

Bowles nodded and he, Alfred, and Joe lifted Charley and began to carry him away. Looking back toward the line, however, Charley whispered,

"My drum."

Joe turned back and spotted it. He ran quickly to where the drum lay and slung it over his shoulder before hurrying back to the others. It took only the two men to carry Charley, so Joe followed alongside them, doing his best to comfort him as they went.

"We'll get you patched up, Charley," he said. "The doctors will know what to do for sure. This is a war, after all. I'm certain they've seen this sort of thing before."

Joe smiled down at Charley, but Charley could see apprehension in the faces of Alfred and Bowles. He tried to speak but he could not find the strength. Instead, he slipped away into the darkness.

When he awoke, he was being lowered onto a cot in a medical tent with Bowles and Alfred standing over him. A doctor approached and looked at the wound with a frown.

"I must return to my unit," Bowles said. "God be with you, Charley."

Charley replied with a weak nod and Bowles hurried off. The doctor was still examining the wound, but Charley could see doubt etched across his face. After a few minutes, he shook his head.

"I'm sorry," said the doctor. "I don't think there is anything we can do. It's gone clear through the body and wreaked havoc the whole way. There's nothing left in there I can fix. I'm sorry, son."

"Nothing?" Alfred spat, "there can't be nothing! Do something, he's… just a boy."

"I'm afraid age makes no difference," the doctor replied. "All we can do is make him comfortable now."

Alfred cast his eyes down to the ground, as the doctor walked away. In the distance, the sounds of battle could still be heard into the evening and eventually faded by nightfall. Charley moved in and out of consciousness as time passed, and though Alfred and Joe tried to speak with him when he woke, he could make only a few quiet replies.

★ ★ ★

The next day, Charley still clung to life. The battle at Antietam did not resume, and when the sun was at its highest point, Captain Sweney appeared in the medical tent. Charley looked up at him through half-closed eyes and could see the pain on his face.

"I'm sorry, Charley," he said. "This wasn't supposed to happen."

Sweney took his hand and knelt beside him. He leaned in close, allowing Charley to whisper in his ear.

"Did we win?" he asked.

Captain Sweney pulled back with a melancholy smile.

"We took the field," he said. "I don't know why McClellan didn't renew the attack this morning. We had the Rebels on their heels, but instead we stood our ground. Lee is retreating across the Potomac as we speak. The men are calling it a victory."

"But you're not?" Charley replied in a whisper.

"I've never seen so many dead and wounded," Captain Sweney confessed. "Ten thousand casualties at least. Well over two thousand of our men dead. Looked to me like we lost more men than they did… I suppose we had more to start with."

Charley nodded.

"I'd like to call it a victory," he said.

"Then that's what it was," Captain Sweney replied. "Charley, I'm so sorry I let this happen. I promised I would keep you safe and I didn't. You're here now because I made a promise I couldn't keep…"

"No," Charley whispered. "I'm here for… same as you… because I believed… in our nation… that hasn't changed."

Captain Sweney nodded, as a tear dropped from his eye.

"It hasn't changed for me either," he said.

"Or me," Alfred added.

"Nor me," Joe said.

"Charley," Captain Sweney said, "I know none braver than you. It was an honor to have you at my command and a pleasure to have you at my side. God bless you, Charley."

With all the strength he could muster, Charley raised his hand and placed it upon the captain's.

"The Union forever, Captain." He coughed, feeling the deep ache in his body as the blood still seeped from his wound. "The Union… forever…"

And with that, he slipped quietly into sleep.

Epilogue

Charley died on September 20, after suffering excruciating pain for three days. His father was stationed some 10 miles away at the time with another regiment and did not receive word in time to see his son before he passed. To this day, it is unknown whether Charley was buried at Antietam or if his body was carried back to West Chester by his father.

A monument was erected in his honor at Greenmount Cemetery where his parents Pennell and Adaline, as well as the man we presume to be his brother, Lewis, are buried. News of Charley's death devastated the Borough of West Chester, and the legacy of his bravery lives on to this day.

Alfred Moulder survived the war. He moved to Sunbury, PA in Northumberland County, where he raised a family and worked as a Railroad Engineer. His brother Townsend is an ancestor of the author of this novel.

Joseph Keene also survived the war and returned to Moscow, PA.

Captain Sweney continued in the Army of the Potomac, becoming a captain in the 20th Pennsylvania Cavalry. He saw the war through to its finish and his regiment was present at Appomattox Courthouse. After the war, he returned to West Chester and became an active member in the Grand Army of the Republic Post 31. He is buried in Greenmount Cemetery with his wife and daughter.

John Coon was captured and died in Andersonville prison along with nearly 13,000 other Union soldiers. Records from Andersonville are not fully reliable, but all evidence points to the fact that his remains are buried there. All told, approximately 56,000 prisoners died in miserable conditions during the Civil War.

Colonel Irwin returned to command the 49th after Antietam. While he was given several commendations by his superior officers following the battle, he remained a colonel for the remainder of his service. He was wounded near Fredericksburg while crossing the Rappahannock River. He and his men were the first to cross the river in a bid to push the Rebels back. Though the wound was not fatal, Irwin decided to resign his commission and return to civilian life.

The regiment was left in the care of Thomas Hulings who rose to the rank of colonel. He led the 49th with distinction in several engagements, earning the admiration of many inside and outside the regiment. He fought bravely during General Grant's Overland Campaign and was killed in battle at Spotsylvania. He left behind a wife, Mary.

Lieutenant Wombacker survived the war, though he was wounded during the Overland Campaign. He served with distinction, being promoted to captain after the battle of Fredericksburg. He would later be promoted to major in August 1864 and lieutenant colonel in April 1865 after being wounded for a second time. He and his wife Emma lived out their days in Luzerne County, PA.

Don Juan Wallings left the 49th in early 1863 but reenlisted three more times before being honorably discharged at the rank of captain in 1866. He was married after the war and moved about from place to place. He lived for a time in Atlantic City, NJ, where he ran a hotel, before moving back to the Philadelphia area. That time was spread between Clifton Heights, Columbia in Lancaster County where he worked as a sign artist, and various other areas. He and his wife are buried at Greenwood Cemetery in the City of Lancaster.

The Civil War continued for three more years, and over 600,000 men, black and white, slave and free, Northern and Southern, were killed in the conflict—either in action, as a result of wounds, or by disease. When civilian deaths are added, the total rises above a million.

It remains the bloodiest conflict ever to touch American soil.

Acknowledgments

I would like to express my appreciation for the many people who helped to make this book a reality. My father and my brother were instrumental in the initial editing of the book. I would not have known about Charley were it not for Bob McGonigal, and I certainly would never have finished the Eagle project that inspired this book without him, my parents, and my fellow scouts from Troop 51 in East Brandywine. Finally, I must also thank my wife for her constant loving care, my sister for her support, and the many diligent people at Brookline and Casemate Publishers for bringing this book to print.